Karl Pieber / Peter Modl

Espalier Fruit Trees
For Wall, Hedge, and Pergola

INSTALLATION • SHAPING • CARE

Schiffer Publishing Ltd

4880 Lower Valley Road • Atglen, PA 19310

Designed by Molly Shields
Type set in ITC Symbol/ Univers-CondensedLight
Cover Designed by Justin Watkinson
ISBN: 978-0-7643-4488-6
Printed in China

Published by Schiffer Publishing, Ltd.
4880 Lower Valley Road
Atglen, PA 19310
Phone: (610) 593-1777; Fax: (610) 593-2002
E-mail: Info@schifferbooks.com

For our complete selection of fine books on this and related subjects, please visit our website at www.schifferbooks.com. You may also write for a free catalog.

We are always looking for people to write books on new and related subjects. If you have an idea for a book, please contact us at proposals@schifferbooks.com.

Schiffer Publishing's titles are available at special discounts for bulk purchases for sales promotions or premiums. Special editions, including personalized covers, corporate imprints, and excerpts can be created in large quantities for special needs. For more information, contact the publisher.

Originally published as Spalierobst für Mauer, Hecke, Pergola ... Anlegen • Formen • Pflegen
© Copyright by Leopold Stocker Verlag, Graz 2011: ISBN 978-3-7020-1308-0. Translated by Omicron Language Solutions, LLC.

Contents

Introduction

In recent years, people's desire to alter the layout of their gardens has again gained in popularity. Many enjoy the opportunity to design an intimate environment using various methods and to reinvent their gardens over and over again. Although most conform to already proven or familiar ideas, the imagination has no bounds when it comes to gardening. Of course, each respective situation ultimately determines what is possible and how something can be achieved successfully.

The urge to "shape," however, should never disregard a plant's naturalness; shapes and other intrusions should correspond to a plant's natural development. Shapes can serve as ornamentation, like those formed by espaliers, but they can also be useful.

A country manor's inner courtyard, well-shaped using contoured pruning.

For the time being, the not-so-skilled hobby gardener is advised to lean more toward proven methods in order to ease into the subject matter. Later, with increasing certainty and after some success, there is almost no limit to the possibilities.

Of course it is also very helpful to take part in various pruning courses that teach you the basic rules, which can later be implemented into your space.

Fully grown cordon trees in an apple garden.

Attempts to bring plants into certain shapes is not something completely new. Looking back in history, the Greeks as well as the Romans (and surely other cultures) tried to configure garden plants and ornamental plants, such as the cypress and the native boxwood, into various shapes (geometric or animal shapes, for example). During the Baroque period (16th and 17th centuries) in Europe, new garden designs with diverse aspects were developed. Architects were not content with simply constructing level gardens or terraces, installing water basins and canals, and designing curved or straight pathways; every tree and shrub, practically every living part of these gardens, was reduced to some artificial shape.

Even though today's designs clearly deviate, the occasional tendency to use special shapes for trees and shrubs has been preserved. Economic interests certainly play a role too.

Ultimately, it was smaller crown forms found in shaped fruit growing that were the origin and foundation of today's intensive orchard systems.

The experiences gained by growing espalier fruit trees, particularly the use of weaker growing rootstocks, laid the foundation for applications in today's intensive fruit production and for training new crown forms (slender spindle, super spindle, etc.).

Importance and Advantages of Espalier Fruit Trees

The use of weaker growing rootstocks with many fruit varieties today has resulted in several new possibilities for smaller gardens. Fortunately, many garden designers also incorporate hedges, trellises and even pergolas into their creations.

Special shapes, particularly those of fruit trees, present a challenge to the interested hobby gardener, but these shapes also offer some useful advantages.

A shady archway leads to another garden section.

Wall espaliers, which are used primarily to cover bare wall surfaces, definitely have a significant impact. Entwinement around doors and windows can lend a more agreeable appearance to buildings. Planting on walls that radiate heat can also bring precious fruits to ample ripeness in less hospitable climates.

By planting on walls that radiate heat, heirloom fruits are brought to ample ripeness.

With the appropriate fruit species and variety, it is possible to produce quality table fruit with unnatural (artificial) crowns. Of course, proper professional care of the plants is required for success.

Usually, the available space in a garden is limited. Using smaller, specially adapted tree and crown forms, it is possible to plant many different kinds of fruits in a relatively cramped space.

Exceptional quality fruits also grow on cordon trees.

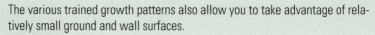

The various trained growth patterns also allow you to take advantage of relatively small ground and wall surfaces.

Adverse weather conditions (such as hail, wind, etc.) also have less impact on small trees, which generally means an earlier harvest and a more regular yearly fruit set.

Espalier fruit trees also manage to produce fruit with the best quality. Pest control measures and effective defenses against springtime frost are easily implemented for the most part. Planting and cultivating different varieties in small areas also offers the fruit lover the opportunity practice their own fruit studies.

For complete success, it is necessary to be properly acquainted with the growing behaviors and fruiting characteristics of each fruit variety used.

For newcomers it is certainly more sensible to begin with simpler forms and to acquire the necessary knowledge for practical use. These acquired experiences also help when choosing varieties and rootstocks later on.

Some Basic Tips

The interested hobby gardener or fruit lover tries to produce fruit and other products of the highest quality possible, even in climatically inhospitable conditions. In many cases, fruit can have some success — mainly early-ripening varieties and, to some degree, in free standing trees. It is futile to hope for an equal yield from the more demanding fruit varieties (like later-ripening fall and winter pears, sensitive apple varieties, but mainly diverse stone fruit varieties). Heirloom varieties often lag behind in their growth, have little color or taste when fully ripe, and also don't keep for long.

> If protective wall, house or fence surfaces are available in such gardens, though, it is quite possible to achieve good fruit harvests, even in unfavorable conditions.

The cultivation of peaches and apricots in such areas is practically impossible since branches and buds of free-standing trees are often battered by low winter temperatures and early blooming is destroyed by late frosts. Protective walls can really work wonders here.

Even early-ripening varieties of grapes, arranged on sunny, south or southwest facing walls, can produce usable grape harvests. Fig trees, which are native to southern Europe, always require winter protection in these climates. But on warm, sunny south-facing walls, you can count on remarkable yields with these trees too.

Before planting can begin on a wall surface, a suitable fruit variety and tree shape (trained growth pattern) should first be determined.

> It is entirely possible to plant on just about any wall surface, but not all fruit varieties prosper equally well on every house or wall surface.

The compass direction that each respective wall faces is particularly important. Warm temperatures are naturally advantageous, but excess solar heat (solar radiation) can negatively affect growth and yield in some fruit varieties. These peculiarities have to be considered when planning your planting. South-facing walls promise success in unfavorable conditions, but other walls (facing southwest, southeast, etc.) should also be taken into consideration before planting.

Excessive sun can negatively affect growth.

SOUTH-FACING WALLS in good and very good conditions are mainly suitable for planting grapes, heirloom pears, various stone fruits (apricots, peaches and nectarines), kiwis and possibly fig varieties.

> Planting apple varieties, on the other hand, should be avoided here since there is a risk of sunburn, but also partly because of the higher risk of disease and pest infestation.

Wall espaliers can dramatically change a house's appearance.

Appropriate apple varieties and even suitable pear varieties can, however, have success at higher altitudes or in other less favorable conditions. Stone fruits, even early-ripening varieties, rarely prosper in such climates. In addition to south-facing surfaces, west- and southwest-facing walls are very good for planting, especially in favorable climates. In addition to pears, apricots, and apples, sweet and sour cherries also do well here.

> Stone fruits rarely prosper at higher altitudes.

In less suitable higher altitudes (above 1,100 yards or 1,000m), only appropriate apple and pear varieties will have success here.

EAST-FACING WALLS, in favorable climates, can be used for planting apple and pear varieties (varieties not ripening too late), but also for more robust plum varieties.

NORTH-FACING WALLS' surfaces, in favorable areas, are definitely suitable for more stable apple varieties and morello cherries. Cultivating red currants would also be possible here.

Otherwise, planting on north walls is not advised. It is important that plants are protected from direct north and northeast winds in order to reduce frost damage as much as possible.

> Apple varieties can also grow on north walls.

These kinds of trained palmetto patterns are only possible on suitable building surfaces.

Support Structures

The prospective design of the support structure, which ultimately plays a part in determining the trained growth pattern of the plant used, is important when making the necessary considerations regarding the installation of espaliers and other forms. Depending on the specific needs, and of course the options, it will be necessary to choose a structure that gives the tree a safe and secure support and can serve as a suitable aid for formation and growth.

> Since these required support structures can, in a way, assume a decorative role (particularly during the vegetation-free period), the surrounding area should be considered when choosing materials.

This should definitely be taken into consideration, especially with espaliers on house walls.

Generally, there are three different espalier categories:
- Wall espaliers in their various forms
- Free espaliers (hedge forms)
- Pergolas (arbors, sitting areas)

Various materials can be used for the construction of the frame or trellis: wood, concrete, glass panels or metal (hardware, wires, etc.). Using glass panels as a barrier, for example, has the advantage of light exposure from two sides as opposed to only one side of a house or barrier wall, which is almost entirely cut off by shadow. This installation, however, is quite a bit more cost intensive compared to other frame materials.

The stability of the framework should correspond to the expected growth rate of the plant and its achievable fruit yield.

The support structure should last as long as the life expectancy of the fruit tree or other plant variety used.

In cooler regions, apricots can only be grown on protective wall espaliers.

Wall Espaliers

Wall espaliers, which are located on suitable house or barn walls and sometimes barrier walls, are not necessarily dependent on the availability of garden space. They are usually planted without front garden space, directly on a path or on the edge of a yard. However, it is advised to make sure that the planting areas (surfaces) are not measured too small (too little open ground) since the roots have to pass at least partly under a sealed ground surface. Adequate soil tilling, fertilization and watering are also complicated in this case.

A good planting here, however, with suitable soil preparation and the use of appropriate plant material (more vigorous, stronger), could help balance out any possible disadvantages.

Before planting, it is necessary to install the required framework (trellis) on the wall surface. A minimum distance of 4 to 6 inches (10-15cm) from the wall should be maintained when mounting the wooden slats. It would be wrong, for example, to attach framework directly on the wall since it would considerably complicate the shaping and stitching of branches, impede the later fruit set, and diminish or prevent essential rear ventilation. Infestation by pests and diseases would increase and make the necessary control measures all the more difficult.

An espalier frame usually has two stronger cross bars (more if necessary), which should be firmly fastened to the respective wall surface (see illustrations on page 17 and 18).

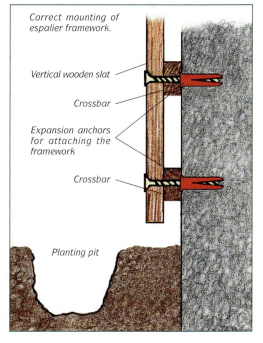

Correct mounting of espalier framework.

Vertical wooden slat

Crossbar

Expansion anchors for attaching the framework

Crossbar

Planting pit

The appropriate distance from the wall is achieved by using an adequately sized spacer or crossbar. Vertical slats (1" to 1-1/2" [25-40mm]) are then attached to the crossbars 9-13/16" to 11-13/16" (25-30cm) apart. Essentially, the gaps between slats are aligned according to the chosen tree shapes (Palmetto-shaped, U-shaped, cordon trees) or according to other trained growth patterns.

Select the spacing according
to the trained growth shape.

If only a simple espalier is to be constructed, the slat distance is not as important. However, if you want to train a fan-shaped espalier, for example, as is common with

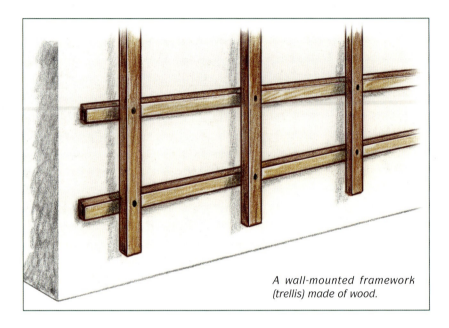

*A wall-mounted framework
(trellis) made of wood.*

Choose a smaller distance
for fan-shaped espaliers.

diverse stone fruits, then the slat distance has to be narrower (5-7/8 to 7-7/8 inches [15-20cm]) so that the branches can attach more easily for the required shaping. Furthermore, painting the framework with plant-compatible substances will extend the life of the framework structure (primarily when using wood).

For a simpler framework layout, constructing a wooden frame with vertical wires would also suffice in some cases. A grid consisting of thin iron rods in a fitted frame could also be adequate.

The wires used should be coated with plastic, however, since galvanized wire corrodes over time, particularly with the use of sulfurous pesticides, and can cause chafe marks on the branches and even breakage of the framework.

Free Espaliers (Fruit Hedges)

Free-standing espalier forms are used primarily in larger gardens for separating differently used plots or to create other boundaries. The framework for such hedges can be made relatively easily and cheaply, but the micro-climatic conditions for the fruit varieties used should be reasonably appropriate and the wind exposure of the areas in question should not be too excessive.

> Fruit hedges are often used to create boundaries.

If a hedge is installed despite negative factors, the framework's bracing has to be stronger and more stable.

A fruit hedge palmetto with horizontally trained side branches.

In order for the fruit tree to achieve the most optimal light exposure possible, these espaliers should be arranged in a north-south direction if possible and should not exceed a certain height (2 to 2.4 yards [1.8-2.2m]). This is similar to the wire trellises commonly found in vineyards.

In order to ensure sufficient stability for hedge espaliers, it is particularly important to use equally sized, stable end posts. These can be made of wood (waterproof logs), concrete (prefabricated reinforced concrete columns) or metal (larger boiler pipes). Because these end posts are stressed the most (mainly when the hedge is completed), an additional inward support or outward bracing is usually necessary. To increase the stability, these end posts should also be set deep enough (23-5/8" to 31-1/2" [60-80cm]) or, with longer rows, cast in concrete.

> Especially important: Stable ends

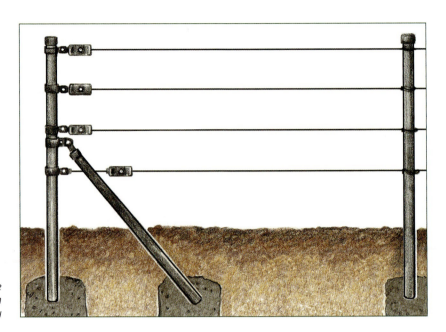

Fruit hedge frame (free espalier) with tubing set in concrete for better stability

To fasten the wires (1/8" [2.5mm], plastic coated), somewhat weaker intermediate supports must be placed at appropriate distances (6-1/2 to 13 feet [2-4m]) depending on the length of the planned span. Thus, a sag in the wires is avoided and more accurate shaping is possible later.

> For best results, the lowest wire (first wire) should be placed at the height of the first branching (no lower than 15-3/4" to 19-3/4" [40-50cm]), and the rest of the wires arranged above it with spacing of 9-13/16" to 11-13/16", but no higher than 15-3/4" (25-30cm/40cm).

Tightening of the wires is then carried out with a simple wire tensioner, which is common in viticulture. If two wires are tightened at the same height (double wire frame), later shaping and fastening of the shoots is made much easier (threading). The already mentioned framework height of 2 to 2.4 yards (1.8-2.2m) should not be exceeded so that all required pruning and care can take place from the ground. A frame with double wires is mainly used for installing grapevine hedges and is very well suited for soft fruits.

If there is enough wood available, the hedge installation can also be made with slats, whereby thin slats are attached vertically on a larger base frame. With the exception of the two supporting crossbars, it is usually no longer necessary to mount more slats.

> If several rows are planned next to one another, the appropriate spacing must be considered due to any possible shade.

A simple wood slat trellis is also adequate for separating small areas

The wind protection effect of a hedge can have a positive impact on the development of lower vegetable or strawberry cultivations in the garden. The various palmetto shapes, Y-shapes, the oblique hedge or the cordon hedge, and irregular fan shapes can be used as trained growth forms. Most fruit varieties are trained in various lengthwise crown forms. Free-standing espaliers can, of course, also be used with other plants, such as rugosa roses, deutzia or berberis. In most cases, only a light frame is required, or none at all with the appropriate pruning measures.

Wind protection effect for vegetables.

Pergolas (Bow-shaped or Rectangular)

When installing a new garden entrance area or walkway, most people have various creeping or climbing plants in mind (mainly roses, clematis, etc.). Fruit trees, though, can be both pleasant and useful in this case. Blooming in spring, green foliage in summer and fruits of varying colors in the fall could be enough incentive to try it out.

Pergolas can be designed very differently, depending on purpose or availability of space. A narrower design over a garden's entrance can be very inviting and decorative, but if the size of the garden allows, larger, rounded shapes or longer archways can also be created.

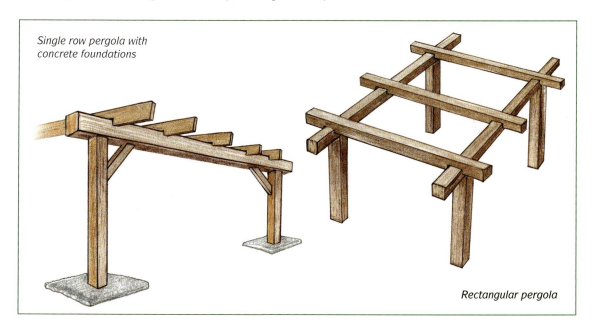

Single row pergola with concrete foundations

Rectangular pergola

A sunny, free space that is preferably unshaded by larger, older trees is a long-term necessity for a pergola.

For better exposure to light, a north-south orientation should be chosen when setting up a pergola. A stable, lasting support apparatus should be used since a heavy strain is put on the upper part by the fruit later on (more so with pome fruits). Thus, appropriately strong wood elements are necessary, including the horizontally positioned wood sections and the supporting elements.

Solid-squared timber, iron pipe, or other applicable structural parts with appropriate bracing wire (for archways) and other wood materials (for the garden entrance area, for example) will be used. Prepared concrete foundations with appropriately arranged linkage for supporting wood or metal elements help extend the life expectancy of the uprights.

A simple roof-shaped frame could also be built using longer pliable stakes. Fastening and stabilization of these supports is later achieved by the tendriled plants (kiwis or grapes, for example). A pergola made of fruit trees (first and foremost to be considered are apples or pears) can be constructed relatively easily as well. Trees are trained as cordon (upright) trees, for example, in two rows over prepared arches or along wires until the tips meet on the top.

Compatible pollination partners should be integrated when planting, unless there is no more available space for other trees.

Whether to design a shorter or longer pergola depends on the corresponding space availability when a number of arches are involved. These forms develop less densely if multiple-armed espalier trees (horizontal palmetto shapes) are used on both sides (see illustration). Pergolas are only effective in gardens with enough space.

A simple pergola designed with logs creates an entryway covered by vines (above)

An arbor decorated with rambler roses (below)

Planting

For the most part, the time for planting fruit trees depends on location and each particular fruit variety. Sometimes it seems that too much importance is attached to the question of whether to plant in the fall or in spring. Usually it is not so much about when to plant, but how to plant that is essential.

> Generally, it can be said that trees or shrubs planted by the fall deadline (from October to the first frost) grow better the following spring since partial enrooting still occurs when the ground temperature is above 32°F (0°C) in the fall.

Also, an ample supply of water should be given in the fall for new root formation. If it is instead first planted in the spring (from March to early May) subsequently followed by a dry period, a growth shock can occur, which can last the entire year. Watering by hand can definitely help, but it does not replace natural precipitation.

Among the most widely used fruit trees, there are some varieties that are more vulnerable to frost due to their pedigree and usually do not enroot during fall planting. Peaches, nectarines, apricots, kiwis and blackberry belong to this group of trees. In addition to frost damage, these fruit varieties can also suffer from irreversible drought damage and lose their ability to grow in the spring if newly formed, absorptive white roots are absent. Therefore, it is more beneficial to plant these trees in the springtime. Very compact, moist and cold soil is also favorable for a spring planting.

Container plants, which are offered in large quantities today, can be bedded out any time of the year.

Performing the Planting

It can not be said often enough that fruit trees normally remain at their intended locations over a long period.

One mistake can be very difficult to correct in most cases, if at all. Therefore, the planting should be well thought out and properly planned.

It is also highly recommended to inform yourself about the pH value of your garden's soil before planting. With high Ca-values in the soil, precautions must be taken for some sensitive fruit varieties (quinces, peaches, etc.). Today there are simple tests (pH indicators, for example) for determining the pH value.

If the planting is planned for a larger area, it is advisable to inform yourself about the specific nutrient levels of the designated soil. Most important here are the somewhat heavier, versatile key nutrients: phosphorous, potassium and calcium. Determining deficiencies at this particular time are even easier to balance out with an appropriate fertilizer. Respective data can be read from the results of the soil analysis.

This two-year-old apple tree in a container with palmetto-trained lateral branches is ready to be planted.

Planting Pit

In the proper soil conditions, the size of the planting pit can be adjusted to the size of the root ball, especially if the soil has already been loosened. If only one tree is intended (at the site of a wall espalier perhaps), then a planting pit should be dug that guarantees the tree the most optimal development possible during its first few years.

Adjust the size of the planting pit according to the size of the root ball!

Replacing soil, or at least mixing soil with a good compost or other suitable organic soil can have quite a positive impact on later growth.

The planting pit can be up to three feet (1m) in diameter with a depth of around 23-5/8" to 31-1/2" (60-80cm). Rodent mesh barriers, which may be necessary, are easier to place in a somewhat larger pit.

If the cultivation layer (active, living soil) is not deep enough (less than 15-3/4" [40cm]), then the plants should not be submerged in the inadequate soil layers. In such cases, it is more advantageous to perform a mound planting on an embankment. After the plants have enrooted, a mound can even be leveled out again and the remaining garden level blended in.

Inserting the Plants

If it appears necessary, place the plants in water or a muddy liquid pulp before planting. This should not exceed six to eight hours with stone fruits. The soaking helps the roots refill the water lost through excavation (naked roots).

When trimming the roots, only the pieces that were damaged during the uprooting process should be removed. Frayed root ends should be cut cleanly.

The active topsoil layer should reach a depth of about 13-3/4" to 15-3/4" (35-40cm).

> It is also important to mix in a bit of excavated soil. When the roots begin to spread later on, even above the planting pit, a growth shock can be prevented.

Loosening the soil of the prepared planting pit also helps the plant develop better later on.

Since espalier fruit trees are usually trained on a frame, the use of plant stakes are normally not required. When planting, the growing point must be located two to four inches (5-10cm) above the surface level, especially with fruit trees. Special attention should also be given to plants that have been grafted at the root neck (shield budding). If the growing point falls below the ground surface, heirloom varieties can "grow free" (form their own roots) and certain characteristics of the base can be lost (weak growing, for example).

The growing point at the neck of the root has to remain 2" to 4" (5-10cm) above the level surface.

When filling the planting pit, it is also important to make sure that the looser, finely crumbled soil comes to rest in the root area in order to ensure a good seal between the ground and the roots. The tree can also be moved from side to side or up and down when filling the planting pit so that hollow spaces between the roots can be prevented. Regular pushing during the planting process decreases the appearance of a "settling" tree.

Well-developed, strong, and healthy roots are required for quick growth.

Finishing the tree bed with watering groove

Filling in the rest of the planting pit and installing a watering groove completes the planting. By watering the plants, any remaining hollow spaces in the roots will eventually be filled in, thereby ensuring an adequate soil to root contact. To protect the planting area from drying out, the tree bed can be covered with organic materials (straw, grass, etc.) as a final step. This covering also helps eliminate the growth of weeds around the tree bed.

Planting Material

Suitable plants can be purchased at practically all brand name tree nurseries. Cultivating your own plants can of course be accomplished, but this requires some knowledge and skills (grafting, etc.). Most nurseries today are happy to take over the maintenance of your plants for a fee. Thus, it is not necessary to conduct complex plant breeding on your own.

> The most convenient way to grow plants is to use one-year-old grafts or, at the most, two-year-old plants.

It is also important that they are free from diseases and pests and don't exhibit any defects (deformities). Virtually every espalier design can be trained from these one- to two-year-old plants.

Rootstocks

Combining the chosen fruit variety with the appropriately fitting rootstock makes planting possible. It also enables a tree's growth and later development to adapt to the respective local conditions and balance out any unfavorable soil conditions that may exist.

> Generatively propagated plants (by seed) or vegetatively propagated plants (by stem cutting, scions, etc.) that are already rooted are referred to as rootstocks. Rootstocks are then grafted to valuable, matching heirloom plant varieties.

Some nurseries offer preformed plants (like the V-shaped plants pictured here), which can also be grown on patios.

The rootstocks you choose should carry specific desired characteristics (growth rate, robustness, fruitfulness, better soil compatibility, susceptibility to disease and cold, etc.) over to the entire plant. Grafting makes it possible to at least partly join the positive characteristics of two partners.

> When choosing rootstocks, there are two factors of crucial importance: soil quality/locational factors and the size of the available wall surface (barrier wall, espalier height, pergola size).

If only a smaller surface area is available for the planned wall espalier, then weaker-growing rootstocks are used. If a bigger wall or barrier surface is being used, though, then grafts are applied to strong-growing rootstocks (seedlings, for example). Stronger-growing rootstocks are also more favorable in lighter soils.

If you intend to grow accurate espalier shapes, weaker-growing variety/rootstock combinations are advised. The appropriate plant spacing must also be considered in order to ensure that the tree grows under optimal conditions as long as possible.

> Weaker growing rootstocks induce earlier fruitfulness, usually produce regular and abundant harvests, and are also easier "to keep in form." These are precisely the characteristics that today's garden fruit grower expects.

Grafts of native seedlings normally grow very strongly, require a lot of care and are ready to harvest much later.

The propagation of soft fruits usually occurs without grafting by using cut stems, scions, offshoots or aided by root seedlings. Only currant or gooseberry tall standard trees are grafted to suitable, root-forming rootstocks (golden currants, for example). Kiwis and grapes can also be grown from grafts.

Propagation of soft fruits usually occurs without grafting.

Apple Rootstocks

Initially, the vegetatively propagated rootstocks (so-called clonal rootstocks), which are used today in tree nurseries, were studied in English research labs for their usefulness and special characteristics.

Probably the most important representative of this group is the **M 9 (Metz Yellow Paradise Apple)**, which is already available in many different selections and new varieties. Due to its breadth of characteristics, it is possible to take almost all locational problems into consideration. It produces early and regular harvests and improves the fruit quality. The trees stay relatively small and are therefore a good fit in smaller gardens. However, this rootstock has somewhat higher ecological demands — it needs good, humic soil that is water and nutrient rich and without stagnant moisture. Its compatibility with other apple varieties is very good. This rootstock is also resistant to collar rot.

M 26 (Crossbreed M 16 x M 9) grows somewhat stronger than M 9 and is therefore better suited for slightly weaker budding varieties. It is also a bit more robust and frost resistant.

M 7 has a stronger growth behavior than M 26 and it is much more stable. It copes with cooler soils quite well and is resistant to collar rot.

MM 106 (Crossbreed Northern Spy x M 1) is average growing, induces early and regular fruitfulness, and is also well suited for lighter soils. It is, however, susceptible to collar rot.

A 2 (Alnarp-Selection): This very adaptable rootstock grows quite vigorously (around 70-80% as measured by the seedling) and it is especially suitable for dry and lighter soils. It has very good stability and a high frost resistance. It also induces early budding and equally early defoliation, which is especially advantageous in climatically unfavorable regions.

Well-rooted M9 rootstock, ready for planting

Seedlings (from robust must varieties like Bittenfelder seedlings) for growing espalier fruit are only used in exceptional cases (very large wall surfaces on barns, for example) and in the lightest soils. The harvest for such grafts arrives very late and is rather irregular; the robustness and frost resistance are quite good though.

Seedlings are rarely used for growing espalier fruit.

Pear Rootstocks

Compared to the apple, the number of pear rootstocks is considerably lower, although cultivation and selection has intensified in the last few decades. However, it is still not very easy for the consumer to purchase new pear rootstocks in tree nurseries.

Quince Rootstocks

Quince rootstocks, which vary in their growth rates, are used today in fruit orchards and in home gardens for training smaller tree forms. They fruit relatively early, but require good, humic soils that are nutrient rich and less calciferous. One disadvantage is that these rootstocks are not compatible with all pear varieties; in such cases, a more agreeable variety (Gellert's butter pear, for example) must be grafted between it.

OHF Rootstocks

OHF rootstocks are frost resistant and compatible.

The OHF rootstocks present another group that is less susceptible to chlorosis and particularly frost resistant. They are also compatible with most productive varieties. The most interesting for pear growing is OHF 69 (Farold 69), an average growing, fertile, compatible, fire blight tolerant rootstock, which has already been widely distributed. Other OHF rootstocks have hardly found their way into nurseries.

Pear Seedlings

Pear seedlings (Kirchensaller Mostbirne, for example) are grown for large tree forms, primarily for less suitable soils. It is very long-lasting, stable and frost resistant, but the quality of the fruit is not always completely satisfactory since they are often small and lacking in taste.

Stone Fruit Rootstocks

Sweet and sour cherries are seldom used for espalier.

Using sweet and sour cherries for espalier fruit growing is very limited. But by breeding new weaker-growing rootstocks, the possible applications have improved considerably. Using new cultivated clones from Germany (**GISELA** and **Weiroot-Forms**, like **GISELA 5** or **Weiroot Nos. 72, 53, 158**) it is quite possible to grow sweet cherry espaliers. These new rootstock clones grow considerably weaker than the previously used Clone **F 12/1**, which also induces very steep (narrow) branch angles. The forms mentioned are also suitable for sour cherries. **St. Lucie cherries (P. mahaleb)** use sour cherry rootstocks, primarily in drier soils.

Peaches and Nectarines

For light to average density soils with a calcium content that is not too high, native seedlings are used; for heavier, colder soils, various plum rootstocks (**Brompton, St. Julien plums**) are used. For very calcium-rich, drier soils, **almond seedlings**, and **peach-almond hybrids** would also be suitable.

Apricots

Native seedlings prove their value in light to average density soils. For heavier soils, plum rootstocks are advised (**INRA 655/2 and Torinel**, among others). In practice, these rootstocks have already proven their worth in free hedge cultivation and the cultivation of pyramidal crown forms. Very low tree forms are accomplished by using the plum rootstock

WAVIT R (in vitro propagation). Very large tree forms, in contrast, are produced using suitable strong-growing **myrobalan** plum rootstocks (Clone 29/c, for example).

Plums and Prunes
These fruits are very limited when training the more demanding espalier forms. If they are used, however, for growing a fan espalier, for example, the previously mentioned apricot rootstocks could be used for most varieties.

Prunes are not so well-suited for espalier.

Well-rooted prune root-stocks arranged according to growth rate.

Other Fruit Varieties

Quince and Medlar
Native forms are usually grown for grafting.

Currants and Gooseberries
When planting currants (red, white and black), rooted cuttings are used; gooseberries, on the other hand, use rooted shoots or scions. As already mentioned, grafted plants are only used for cultivation of standard and tall trees. The **golden currant (Ribes aureum)** is usually used as the rootstock since very few ground shoots develop. With the appropriate pruning, shrubs can also be grown as espalier, with two to three shoots or a short base trunk.

Grapes and Kiwis
Grafted as well as **non-grafted plants** (propagated by stem cutting, for example) are used for planting.

Pruning, Training, and Shaping

Pruning is the most important part of tree maintenance, regardless of whether it concerns an intensively managed orchard or a hobby garden. However, before starting your pruning, you should be familiar with which objectives are achieved with each invasive cut — and you should never lose sight of these envisioned objectives.

Tree Pruning Goals
The quickest development possible of the desired tree shape (crown form) and an early harvest.
Establish and maintain a physiological balance between growth and yield throughout the entire crown area.
Sufficient growth and regular fruitfulness should be as well-balanced as possible, even in espalier fruit tree crowns.
Crown expansion achieved by the appropriate pruning procedures should conform to the existing growing space and, above all, avoid bare spots on leaders and branches.
Grow fruits of the highest quality possible.

Generally, developing crown forms should always be approached with the utmost care and consideration. Severe pruning cuts inevitably lead to a disturbance of balance and should be avoided until later, if possible.

Like all other living plants, fruit trees go through certain life phases: youth phase, prime harvesting phase and old age. The objectives for necessary pruning cuts naturally shift according to the respective age of the tree.

During the youth phase, vegetative growth dominates. Pruning cuts should primarily help to build up strong, highly productive and long-living crowns.

When trees come into the harvesting phase, pruning methods are primarily directed at bringing growth and fruit production into balance.

When a tree is beyond its prime harvesting age and enters old age (vitality reduction) then the lost balance must be reestablished by using severe pruning cuts to support its vitality. Even in shaped fruit tree orchards, the fruitful part of the crown will wander outward and the unproductive inner part of the crown will constantly grow larger if not counterbalanced at the right time.

Shaping aid for making a simple U-design

Timely pruning methods must therefore be introduced to rejuvenate the tree.

Laws of Shoot Growth

The growth and development of fruit trees and shrubs are subject to certain natural laws that can be made use of when pruning and shaping. It is beneficial for those who are acquainted with pruning and training to understand the fundamental relationships that govern plant development.

It will also be easier for the individual to understand the responses to different pruning and shaping tasks and to react accordingly.

In espalier fruit growing, pruning plays a much bigger role than with the cultivation of normal round crown shapes. Therefore, it seems necessary and justifiable to first present some of the fundamentals of shoot growth and shoot stimulation.

Principles of Shoot Growth

The position of branches and shoots within the crown and their angle of inclination determine the rate of shoot growth.

Older palmetto with lateral branches trained at an angle

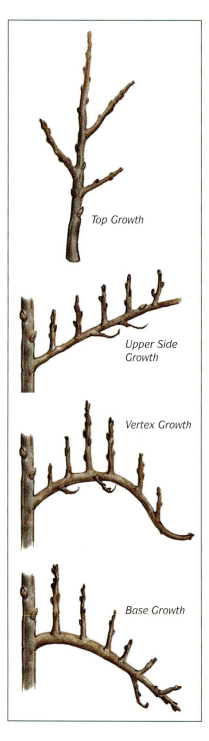

Top Growth

Upper Side Growth

Vertex Growth

Base Growth

Top Growth

The uppermost buds advance more strongly and show the most development. Generally, they possess the highest hormone and nutrient levels and by nature stand quite conveniently next to sap currents. Two or more shoots of the same length and size grow equally strong. Generally, the more angled a shoot is positioned, the more strongly it grows outward — the more level its position, the shorter the growth.

Upper Side Growth

Buds located on the upper side of relatively horizontal shoots or slightly angled shoots sprout fairly uniformly from the contact point to the end.

Vertex Growth

On limbs and branches bent downward by fruit weight (or by shaping), the strongest new shoots develop in the vertex zone. Development at the base and the end lags behind.

Base Growth

The lower a shoot is bent or forced downward, the more the base comes into a favorable (higher) position, which promotes stronger growth.

> Pruning, fastening, and shaping are very common in shaped fruit tree growing. Knowledge of these general rules is therefore very important.

Principles of Pruning

The removal of small or large plant parts by snipping and cutting in the crown has a certain impact on a fruit tree's further development and fruitfulness.

> Assimilates (reserves that are stored in branches), for example, or assimilation surfaces (leaves lost during lopping) are removed, which also affects root development to a certain extent.

Timing also plays an important role in pruning. Shoot growth can be measurably influenced or regulated by it.

Tips for Pruning One-Year-Old Shoots

a) No pruning; the well-formed terminal bud will grow out strongly (top growth)

b) The buds below the terminal bud are weaker, thus weaker growth takes place with many shorter shoots in flatter positions

c) Severe pruning up to the middle of a shoot with well-formed buds means a stronger growth flush with fewer new shoots rising at an angle.

d) Pruning to the area of a shoot base (stub cut) with weaker formed buds brings about weak to average growth flush and very short shoots (vitality reduction)

a)   b)   c)   d)

When to Prune

Winter Pruning

In general, fruit trees and shrubs are pruned during the vegetation-free period (winter). Training tasks (heading, converting, thinning out, rejuvenating, etc.) are generally reserved for this period.

Training tasks are often performed in the winter.

Advantages of Winter Pruning

- A better view of the crown in a defoliated state (fewer pruning mistakes)
- No hanging fruit, which can be obstructive at times
- Free time: the work can be spread out over a longer period

Training mistake: pruning now can rapidly affect the trees in a negative way.

Timely lopping makes shaping easier.

Individual fruit varieties are sensitive to different pruning methods, however.

> While pome fruits and soft fruits tolerate pruning in winter, different stone fruit varieties should be pruned at winter's end instead, or even starting in the summer.

Wounds also heal considerably better during the vegetation period.

Summer Pruning

Summer pruning is carried out during the vegetation period when trees are leafy. Winter pruning procedures should be completed or corrected at this time, and if necessary, undesirable developments counterbalanced. At the same time, stronger growing trees can be balanced out by removing assimilation surfaces (leaves) and the formation of fruit spurs can be facilitated. Pruning in the summer also reduces the time and effort for winter pruning.

> In espalier and shaped fruit tree growing, summer pruning is absolutely necessary for further buildup of the crown.

Pruning helps to guide natural growth in desired paths and supports the formation of flower buds at a very early point in time. Generally, fruit trees develop much longer shoots in the first few years, which are needed for the composition of the crown. This excess of shoots then has to be removed again the following winter. It is therefore more advantageous to remove these growths in the summer by simply breaking them off. Such wounds usually heal quickly and without difficulty. Any remaining shoots can have their ends removed where necessary, which will contribute to flower bud formation through the surplus of nutrients. End removal might also be required several times, primarily when the formation of terminal buds on the end of shoots is delayed.

> In order to aid in the transformation of leaf buds into flower buds, the correct time to prune (pinching) must be chosen.

Studies have shown that the right time for many fruit varieties is just before or at the beginning of flower bud differentiation. With most major fruit varieties, shoot composition gives an overview of the approximate time.

Flower Bud Differentiation of Some Fruit Varieties	
Fruit Variety	Approximate Time
Apple	July to August
Pear	July to August
Prune	Beginning of July to mid August
Sweet cherry	End of June to second half of July
Sour cherry	End of June to end of July
Apricot	July to beginning of August
Peach	Beginning of July to mid August
Currant (red, white)	Mid June to end of July
Grape	Mid June to end of July

Advantages of Summer Pruning
- Growth reduction
- Improved exposure to light
- Positive fruit development and quality improvement
- Ease of crown formation

Shoot and Bud Forms

To prune efficiently, precise knowledge of the different elements of the crown is, to some degree, required. Thus, mistakes can be avoided and pruning can be carried out more easily.

This loosely configured palmetto crown with horizontally-trained branches requires little pruning.

Shoot Forms

Long Shoots (Wood Shoots)
These are usually year old shoots that attain a length of at least 9-13/16" (25cm) and are found on the top of lead shoots. On pome fruit trees these shoots are normally occupied by leaf buds, out of which longer or shorter shoots can develop. Water sprouts present a special form. These are also year old long shoots, which can emerge out of dormant buds in older wood that is several years old. Severe pruning and permanent lack of light can strongly encourage their formation. Water sprouts rarely develop on stone fruit trees though.

Water sprouts emerge out of dormant buds in wood that is several years old.

Short Shoots
Short shoots attain a length of between 6" and 9-13/16" (15-25cm) and also only have leaf buds to start with. They feature a relatively small and narrow pointed shape.

Premature shoots are sprouts that develop from the buds of a new growth flush in the same year. This is a normal development with peaches.

Fruiting Shoots

These are year-old or older branches (shoots), which, in addition to vegetative buds (leaf buds), are also occupied by flower buds. One can differentiate between long and shorter fruit spurs here:

Fruiting shoots are occupied by leaf and flower buds.

Fruiting Canes

Year-old long shoots, more than 9-13/16" (25cm), with a flower bud on the end and leaf buds arranged on the side are referred to as fruiting canes.

Fruiting Spurs

Year-old short shoots, 1-1/2" to 4" (4-10cm), with a terminal flower bud as well as outlying side leaf buds.

Fruiting Scion

These are shorter shoots, less than 2" (5cm), usually with a flower bud positioned on the end. When fruit is too abundant and hanging, the formation of flower buds can stall.

Portion of an older, horizontal birch cordon with various fruiting spurs.

Whorls

These are heavily branched fruiting spurs that are several years old and are only found on pome fruit trees. They include fruiting scions, curly spurs and fruit stalks. Curly spurs are among the several-years-old fruiting spurs and can develop from spurs and scion. The peculiar curled appearance of short shoots originates from the leaf scars of fallen leaves. Fruit stalks (preferred by pears) are the fleshy, thickened part on the end of a fruiting spur or scion, which serve as storage for miscellaneous nutrients. New, short fruiting spurs can form here.

Whorls are comprised of fruiting scions, curly spurs and fruit stalks.

Bouquet Shoots

These are year-old or multiple-year-old fruiting spurs of stone fruits, predominantly found on cherry trees. They are very similar to curly spurs in their development. A series of flower buds arranges itself around a centrally located leaf bud, which serves as the shoot elongation. These shoots can often become many years old.

Bouquet shoots are similar to curly spurs.

True and False Fruiting Shoots

■ **True fruiting** shoots are usually one-year-old long shoots with strong mixed bud placement (with double and triple buds), which form on various stone fruit varieties and are considered important fruit spurs. They are usually encountered on peach trees.

■ **False fruiting** shoots are usually weaker, ill-nourished long shoots that don't exhibit any mixed bud placement. They feature only a leaf bud at the top and flower buds on the sides. They should be removed when pruning. They are primarily found in sparsely pruned peach and sour cherry crowns.

The fruiting stage of an apple tree with a vegetative shoot to extend the fruiting shoot

Bud Forms

Every new development of shoots within the crown results solely from buds. After their placement, **end buds** (terminal buds) and lateral buds are distinguishable. After they form, **leaf** and **flower buds** can be distinguished.

In pome fruits, flower buds are also referred to as mixed buds because they can develop vegetative parts (leaves and short shoots) as well as generative parts (six to ten flowers).

These mixed buds are important in shaped fruit tree growing and for the training of lower forms of pome fruit trees.

With stone fruits, either vegetative buds (leaf buds) or flower buds form. Several flowers (up to four) can develop from flower buds.

Sleeping Buds

Sleeping buds are those that don't sprout the year after their formation. They usually sit at the base of various shoots and remain completely capable of producing shoots. By lightly cutting above the eye they can be stimulated to grow.

Heading Cut

Thinning Cut

Conversion

Pruning Terminology

Before committing to the training of individual crown forms, some pruning terms are explained, which will perhaps make the procedures more understandable.

Heading Cut

A heading cut is the clipping of a year-old shoot above an appropriate leaf bud, which generally points in the desired direction of shoot elongation. It is very important for the build up of the crown.

Thinning Cut

A thinning cut is the removal of unusable shoot material (competitive shoots, for example). Pruning takes place on the contact point.

Bench Cut

A shoot is removed up to an appropriate, lower lying lateral shoot (with shoot elongations growing at an acute angle, for example).

Conversion

A bench cut is referred to as a conversion if the stem elongation is reclaimed by a lower lying shoot.

Pinching

Pinching is the removal of the top part of a not yet ligneous shoot during the vegetation period. It can be performed on a shoot several times if the growth of the shoot has been limited. The shoot's end is pinched off with the fingernails or with pruning shears, whereby the older, assimilated leaves (3 to 4) are preserved. The assimilates reproduced here will be used to form flowering buds or secondary growth of the shoot.

Lorette Pruning

A summer pruning method developed in France, which was originally used on pear trees. All wood shoots that have reached the size of a pencil are cut back beginning in July to lengths of 3/8" to 3/4" (1-2cm). Pruning is carried out routinely until about mid-September, which enhances fruitfulness to a certain extent. This method was also known as stub pruning, but ultimately the name did not catch on. A combination of the two summer pruning methods is definitely beneficial.

Lorette pruning was originally used on pear trees.

Pinching

Lorette Pruning

Conversion

Trained Growth Forms (Espalier Shapes)

In order to produce the desired espalier shapes, the natural development of trees must be radically disrupted.

Bringing the crown into a desired shape is attempted in part by pruning, but also aided by training young and still bendable branches.

Over the years, a number of new espalier designs have been developed, all of which build upon a few basic patterns.

The growth behavior of diagonally trained cordon trees is controllable.

Cordons

Cordon shapes are mainly used with apple and pear trees, but can, of course, also be applied to other fruit varieties (sweet cherries, for example). Depending on the given circumstances, one can distinguish between the various designs: the vertical cordon, a single trunk or two or more parallel growing trunks (U-shapes), the horizontal cordon, the diagonally-trained cordon trees, and other trained growth forms.

Cordon designs are mainly used with apple and pear trees.

Vertical Cordon (Super Spindle)

This is a tree form close to that found in nature, which consists of a short trunk and stem elongation with short fruiting spurs. This form is reasonably simple to train and therefore also well-suited for the less proficient gardener.

The rootstocks used are weak to medium-strength growing clones. Stronger growing rootstocks are only warranted for less suitable soils. Vertically trained cordons grow reasonably quickly and can reach a height of 9-1/2 feet (3m) after only four to five years. However, they require supports for the life of the plant.

Cultivation is relatively simple. One-year-old grafts are the most suitable for the planting. After planting, the shoot is shortened to about 19-3/4" (50cm) and the future stem is attached to the framework.

> Plant spacing of 19-3/4" (50cm) should be maintained for larger plantings in order to ensure sufficient fruiting spur development later.

If adorned (filled with lateral shoots) young trees (container products, for example) are used, the remaining lateral shoots must be shortened or at least formed in a horizontal position.

When using weak rootstocks, very little to no flowers should be left in the first year (planting year). In the following years the fruit set can be slowly increased in accordance with the growth behavior.

The earlier the harvest is initiated, the more the growth of the tree will be influenced and the less time and effort will be dedicated to pruning.

If more buds sprout than are needed for adornment, then they should be broken off in a green phase.

> Ideally, all 6" (15cm) of a new shoot will form on the stem elongation. If these lateral shoots grow too abruptly erect, then a horizontal brace is absolutely necessary during the herbaceous phase.

Cordon tree after winter pruning. The focus is on the development of short fruiting spurs.

Cordon trees of varying growth rates require especially accurate pruning.

If these branches get too long despite shaping more than 9-13/16" to 11-13/16" (25-30cm), then they have to be pinched (end removed). Make sure that the axil buds of the remaining leaves are pointing down and outward.

In accordance with the law of upper side growth, buds sprout out stronger and more abrupt on the upper side of a branch than those arranged on the side or bottom. Therefore, it is important in the first few years to constantly control shoot growth during the vegetation period and, if necessary, correct shoot growth with the appropriate pruning measures (pinching). End removal is no longer required if the shoot indicates that it has completed its growth through the formation of a terminal bud.

> In the first few years after planting, it is usually necessary to deal with stem elongation too. Normally, pruning occurs about 15-3/4" (40cm) above the last lateral shoot.

The more uniformly the lateral shoots develop on the axis, the longer the stem elongation can be left alone. Also, shoots pinched in the first year can be cut back in the spring time near the first pinching, if necessary. Unwanted lateral shoots should be completely removed though. Otherwise, the necessary pruning and training corrections are resumed on the new shoots in order to ensure uniform adornment with short fruiting spurs.

These corrective tasks are also performed during the third year, the same way they were carried out in the first few years. When the tree eventually reaches the desired height, the top will be diverted to a suitable lower lying lateral shoot. In addition, growth will decelerate by the slowly arriving harvest and branches will be forced down horizontally by the weight of the fruit.

IMPORTANT:

To later ensure a suitable balance between vegetative and generative development, it is essential to begin pruning at the right time.

Horizontal Cordons

Horizontal cordon trees are often used for bordering garden and flower beds. They can be very fruitful and produce very good quality fruit. They are also great for covering lower walls.

Horizontal cordons can be trained with a single arm or two arms onto wire frames that reach 15-3/4" to 19-3/4" (40-50cm) above the ground. As a plant product, a one-year-old graft is most suitable. After planting, it is pruned to the appropriate height. In order to

> ## IMPORTANT:
>
> **The appropriate spacing between plants should be maintained. This should be at least 9-3/4 to 13 feet (3-4m) when using medium-strength growing combinations, and 8 to 9-3/4 feet (2.5-3m) with weak growing rootstocks.**

ensure the growth of the cordon, at least in the beginning, the terminal ends should be erect. In late summer, before the lignification of the shoots is completed, they must be formed horizontally again.

In order to guarantee growth, the end bud should point up.

One disadvantage of this training method has proven to be the stronger growth on the upper side of the cordon, mainly near the base (stem). In order to guarantee consistent development on the entire length of the cordon, it is necessary to continuously remove new shoots that are too thick (best carried out by tearing off) and quickly converting the remaining shoot growths into adequate fruiting spurs by using the appropriate methods (pinching, pruning, etc.).

> Accurate and timely execution of these tasks ensures uniform development in the first few years of the cordon.

After achieving the desired length, the top is simply repositioned to a reasonable side shoot and uniform development is maintained through the appropriate pruning tasks.

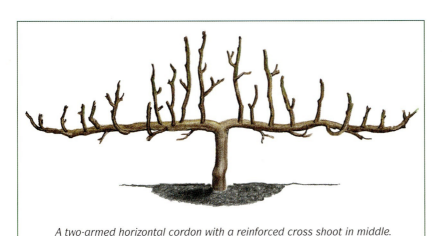

A two-armed horizontal cordon with a reinforced cross shoot in middle.

Two-armed, horizontal cordon with uniform growth and corresponding fruiting spurs.

Two-armed trained growth forms show somewhat better growth rate dispersion.

Data has shown that these cordons are good for the apple varieties: "White Transparent," "Charlamowsky," "Red Fall Kalvill," "Kaiser Alexander," "Ananas Reinette," "Berner Rosen," "White Winter Kalvill," "Baumann's Reinette," and the pear varieties: "Clapp's Favorite," "Williams Pear," "Double Philippe," "Winterdechant," and "Gute Luise." Other fruit varieties, such as prunes or apricots, are not suitable. Sweet cherries would possibly be worth a try with weaker rootstocks.

Oblique Cordons

This form, like the vertical cordon, consists of a straight stem elongation, but is bent at a 45-degree angle. Oblique cordon trees are also trained on framework (3-4 wires) or a wall with the appropriate fastening equipment to heights of up to 9-3/4 feet (3m). These are very well suited for apples as well as pears. The plant width is normally 1-3/4 to 1-9/8 feet (0.5-0.6m).

> Compared to the vertical cordon, the fruitfulness of this tree is initiated somewhat earlier since the bent position and the longer length of the stem encourages the formation of flower buds.

Pruning and maintenance chores are similar to vertical cordons. When the height of the tree reaches the uppermost wire and the leader grows over it, it should be cut back 6" to 7-7/8" (15-20cm) below the upper wire in late spring. By shortening new shoots in July/August every year to about 1" or 2.5cm (Loretta pruning), the diagonally trained cordon trees can maintain this shape over a longer period.

If an oblique cordon tree exhibits growth that is too strong despite all pruning interventions, growth could be abated by additional lowering of the axis. But such measures can only be executed slowly and gradually (3–5° per work cycle) with older trees. In total, lowering to around 35° is possible (illustration page 47).

Diagonally trained cordons also require stable framework.

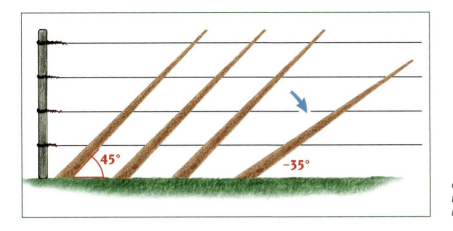

Oblique cordons that grow too strongly can be abated by lowering them to 35°.

Winter pruning of trained cordon trees is good for removing or thinning out old, shabby fruiting spurs that are too thick.

At the same time, existing new shoots are shortened to 3-4 eyes; shoots that continue to grow after pinching are shortened to 1-2 eyes.

During later abatement of growth, severe thinning out and cutting back is carried out to encourage the new formation of young shoots, which are then handled as already described in the summer.

Thinning out and heading reduces growth.

Serpentine Cordons

A serpentine cordon (a special form) requires a template made of adequately strong wire that is attached to the existing framework in order to ensure uniform growth.

The fruitfulness of this trained growth pattern arrives somewhat earlier due to the repeated bending of the tree and the accumulation of sap currents.

This leads to stronger formation of well-supplied flower buds and subsequently to the formation of quality fruit. Because of the earlier appearance of lateral buds, it is also no longer necessary to cut back the top area every year since ample spurring of the axis is assured.

Leads to the formation of quality fruit.

One-year-old grafts on weak to medium-strength rootstocks are used for the planting. The plant width (31-1/2" or 80cm) should not be too narrow so that later development of fruiting spurs is not impaired.

Serpentine cordons are characterized by slow growth and early fruitfulness.

The stem height of this design is about 15-3/4" (40cm). After adequate fastening to the framework, the shaping can then begin. Maintenance and pruning are similar to the already mentioned cordon shapes. It is also possible to plant lower plots (less than 9-3/4 feet or 3m).

With a strong growing cordon, a second tier can be trained.

U-shaped Cordons

Simple U-shape

Training the simple U-shape requires at least one year longer, but has the advantage of shared tree growth on two separate vertical cordons, which can lessen the amount of pruning needed.

For planting, one-year-old grafts on medium-strength rootstocks are best. After the plant reaches a height of about 15-3/4" (40cm) it is pruned back to two eyes. These buds should point in the direction of the espalier to make shaping easier when growing.

After the growth flush, these two herbaceous shoots will be fastened on the right and left at approximately a 45-degree angle. Further shoots that may have formed must be consistently removed for the time being. In the summer (around the beginning of August) both shoots are shaped horizontally before they have completely lignified and the tops, provided that their lengths suffice, are propped up on applicable framework parts.

In order to ensure accurate shaping, the shoots must be fastened to the framework directly before the bend area. Should the angle not be completely attained during the initial shaping, it must be corrected again later.

To prevent a break of partly lignified shoots, they should be bent lightly.

The spacing between the two cordons is generally 15-3/4" or 40cm (corresponds to slat spacing).

To attain uniform development for both stem elongations, they must each be cut at an equal height – that means the tops always have to be at the same height (law of top growth!).

The pruning length must therefore always conform to the weaker stem elongation.

In the following years, both stem elongations and the development of the necessary fruiting spurs are handled in the same way as already described for vertical cordons. The lateral shoots can reach a length of 7-7/8" to 11-3/4" (20-30cm), but should not become longer in order to ensure proper exposure to light. In addition to pinching, second year pruning has proven successful when growing shorter fruiting spurs.

Pruning of a one-year-old shoot to two adequate buds

When shaping, the shoots must be fastened to the framework directly before the bend area.

Cut back to a bud that is pointing upward and in the second year cut back to a suitable, downward-pointing, weaker fruiting branch.

Double U-Shape

At least two to three years are needed for the formation and growth of a double U-shape. The first branching can be arranged a bit lower here so that the bases of both U-shapes can begin at a height of 15-3/4" to 19-3/4" or 40-50cm (framework preparation).

Top left and bottom left: By using shaping aids, it is relatively easy to develop U-shapes with different fruit varieties. Right: By distributing growth on to two cordons, stronger root-stocks can also be used.

IMPORTANT:

Let the first bend run as vertically as possible on the U-base of the cordon. Imbalance can lead to disproportionate development later.

Later corrections are virtually impossible. The cordons are trained further at equal lengths on the vertical espalier slats. Further care (pruning) of the four vertical cordons is then carried out as previously described. The plant width here, including the specified cordon spacing of 15-3/4" (40cm), amounts to 63" (160cm). Since the growth distribution in this case has an even stronger effect, the use of stronger growing rootstocks is advised.

Double U-shapes are, for the most part, decorative forms. Fruit varieties that are well suited for this shape are apple trees and pear trees. They could, however, also be used with sweet cherries or with some prune varieties.

Later corrections are virtually impossible with the double U-shape.

A certain weakening of growth can be achieved by training double U-shapes, but more time must be estimated for cultivation.

Palmettos

Palmetto crowns are among the largest espalier forms.

They feature a straight central leader, from which several horizontally or diagonally-growing lateral branches elevate over one another in tiers -- all existing in the same flat plane.

The number of tiers usually ranges from one to five, but more are definitely conceivable. To ensure appropriate growth, medium to strong-growing rootstocks should be used. On lower barrier walls or small wall surfaces, weaker growing rootstocks are also sufficient.

Palmetto shapes are suitable for apples, pears, sweet cherries, and many prune varieties, but these demanding forms are less suitable for stone fruits, such as peaches, apricots, and sour cherries.

Medium to strong-growing rootstocks should be used to ensure appropriate growth.

Pruning a one-year-old graft to three acceptable buds at the end of winter.

In such cases, designing a fan-shaped crown (common, irregular espalier) turned out to be markedly better.

> Palmetto espaliers, like all more demanding forms, require proper support – whether they are trained on a house or barrier wall or as free-standing hedges on a system of columns and wires.

The height of the furring on the wall, or the spacing of the slats or wires on the framework, should correspond to the espalier levels (15-3/4" to 19-3/4" [40-50cm] spacing).

A one-year-old graft is best for planting (preferably in the fall) and, when it reaches a height of 15-3/4" to 19-3/4" (40-50cm), it is pruned to three healthy buds (pictured left). The shoot of the uppermost bud forms the stem elongation; the two other shoots are trained for the formation of the lower lateral branches. All other forming shoots, primarily in the stem area, should be removed for now.

If the graft intended for planting already has premature shoots, two reasonably positioned side shoots springing up at a stem height of 15-3/4" to 19-3/4" (40-50cm) can be chosen. Immediately attaching them diagonally to the espalier at about a 45-degree angle and cutting them back by one-third to a half in equal lengths is quite advantageous for further development. The stem elongation should then be pruned back about 11-3/4" to 15-3/4" (30-40cm) above the highest positioned lateral shoot to a bud pointing outward. The developing elongation is then fastened to the framework.

In the summer of the first year, the designated stem elongation can also be attached to a post in order to attain good height. The sprouts of the two diagonally attached lateral shoots will be left in this position for now since immediate horizontal training would slow growth too much.

> If the development is still unbalanced despite this, regulation of shoot growth can be achieved by lowering the stronger shoots or by lifting weaker shoots relatively lightly.

In late summer, both lateral shoots (provided that a palmetto shape with horizontal lateral shoots will be trained) are carefully placed in a horizontal position and fastened to the respective framework. If growth turns out to be altogether weak, it should be shortened by at least one-third during winter pruning.

To build up the next tier, the stem elongation is again cut at the end of winter about 15-3/4" to 19-3/4" (40-50cm) above the base branch (first tier).

Older, well-structured palmette with diagonally trained branches (five tiers).

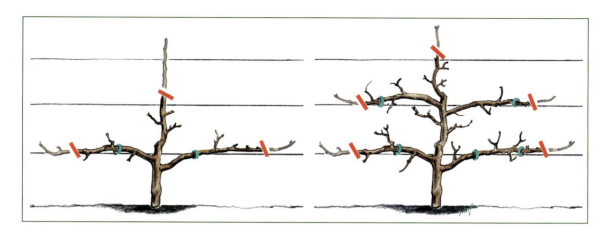

Three well-developed buds should also be available here.

With new growth flushes during the next year (second year of cultivation), the second tier will be trained in a similar way. During the summer months, the lead shoots (as already described with the formation of the first tier) will first grow at a 45° angle and then in late summer or early fall, lowered to the height of the second wire before lignification is complete.

Pruning and fastening at the beginning of the second year (left) and third year (right).

Palmette with one tier (left) and two tiers (right).

With weaker growth, the shoots are shortened. This can be repeated in the same way until the desired number of tiers is reached (see illustration on p. 51).

> If the tree's crown is fully developed, it is important to thwart and correct undesirable developments in the following years using the appropriate pruning methods.

Essential pruning chores are carried out during the summer months (Lorette pruning). Lateral branches with complete shoot growth that are longer than 9-7/8" (25cm) are cut back to three to four leaves above the leaf rosette. Thinning out thick fruiting spurs in winter is most beneficial. The stem elongation and long lateral shoots are shortened at the end of winter.

The palmette is pruned primarily in the summer.

Palmettes with Diagonally Trained Lateral Branches

This form is especially well suited for the less experienced fruit lover since pruning and training are relatively easy to perform.

For the planting, one-year-old grafts with early sprouts are best. A stem height of about 19-3/4" (50cm) is chosen for all forms and lower positioned sprouts are removed immediately in this area. From the remaining lateral shoots, two suitable opposing shoots are chosen and fastened at an angle of about 45° on the supporting framework. To ensure an appropriate growth flush, they are cut back by about one-third of their length.

Complete palmetto crown with five tiers before pruning.

IMPORTANT:

It is imperative that the cut takes place in the sap zone to ensure uniform growth flush.

The stem elongation (central leader) will also be cut about 15-3/4" (40cm) above the contact point of both lateral shoots. Three well developed buds should be found in this area, which will then form the contact points for the next tier. If the first shoots have already formed on the lateral shoots of the first tier during the planting year, they should have their ends removed to a length of 4" to 6" (10-15cm). If more shoots follow out of the shoots with removed tops, it is advantageous to cut back again to one to two leaves. These lopping tasks are then carried out with every other tier.

With strong sprouting of both the lateral shoots and the stem elongation (greater than 23-5/8" to 27-1/2" [60-70cm]), the development of the second tier can already begin. The central leader is pruned like it was in the first year and then the two lateral shoots are cut back far enough so that they collectively form a plane. This normally guarantees that the buds sprout equally strongly.

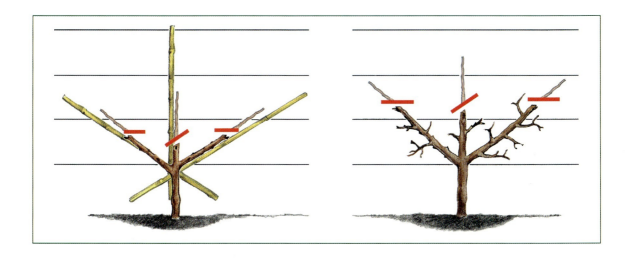

After planting, the lateral shoots are cut back by a third (left). Pruning the shoots in the second year (right).

In such cases, the central leader is again cut back to an eye that is pointing forward and both lateral branches should be pruned back to this height as well. Thus, a uniform growth flush of all shoots is assured.

Individual tiers can now be built up in this pattern until the final crown height is achieved. The central leader is no longer needed with the last tier. Only the two lateral shoots are grown (illustration below).

A fully grown palmetto crown with diagonally trained lateral branches and ample fruit spurring

The Belgian Fence

This hedge design, sometimes also referred to as the crossover espalier or skewed double cordon espalier, can be regarded as the forerunner to the high-density planting systems found in intensive orchards. This pattern can be grown on walls and barriers, but can also very easily be grown as a free-standing hedge for fenced enclosures (illustration below). The basic design constitutes a palmette that has only two diagonally-trained lateral

---

IMPORTANT:

When creating a free-standing hedge, adhering to a north-south direction ensures uniform exposure to sunlight for both hedge sides.

The basic design is the palmette.

Two buds must be situated side by side.

branches. By spacing the plants closely, the diagonal branches cross over one another, contributing to the plant's improved stability.

To cultivate a Belgian fence, either one-year-old grafts or pre-prepared apple and pear saplings are used. To ensure accurate shaping, it is necessary to install the appropriate framework (wire frame) before planting.

When planting one-year-old Okulanten, or during subsequent pruning, make sure that two appropriate, opposing buds are located in a suitable position. These are designated for the future cultivation of lead branches. Plant spacing is 19-3/4" to 31-1/2" (50-80cm).

Pruning work can be kept at a minimum during the planting year. Both newly formed shoots are fastened to the wire espalier at a 45° angle and can intersect at the bottom.

Intersecting the branches improves stability.

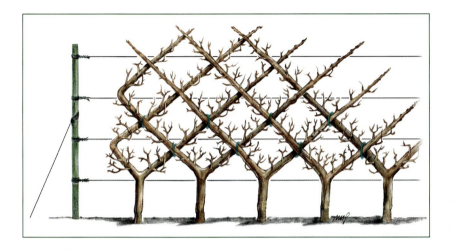

A well-designed Belgian hedge can also serve as a privacy screen.

In the second year, both cordons, depending on the growth rate of each, will be cut back by about one-half. The new growth will then be trained in the same direction. Pruning in the third year is similar to that of the previous years. Normally, this kind of hedge design is complete by the fourth or fifth year at the latest (illustration above).

Pruning the lateral shoots on both main branches is similar to that of the diagonally trained palmette.

On the spots where the branches intersect, merging the cordons can be induced by cutting light gashes (surface wounds) and subsequently bonding them together. This procedure is known as inarching.

This merging can greatly increase the stability of this hedge formation. This design has been used with various pear varieties, such as Amanlis Butter Pear, William Christ, Gute Luise, Gellert's Butter Pear, Duchesse Angoùlème, Diel's Butter Pear, etc. Medium-strength quince rootstocks were used together with the appropriate soil conditions.

Merging branches facilitates stability.

The Candelabra Palmette (Verrier Palmette)

This special espalier form from France is among the largest crown forms and can have any number of branches. By combining several intertwined and intersecting U-shapes, it takes on the shape of a large candelabra. An espalier with three to six double arms has proven to be the most practical.

It can be used with any number of branches.

An even number of branches should always be maintained, though, in order to avoid an unbalanced central axis, which can unfavorably affect development.

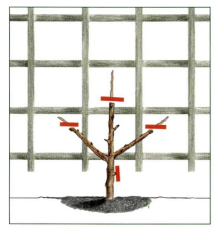

The stem elongation is also pruned back.

If higher walls need to be covered, fewer branches are used, with lower surfaces or barriers, more lateral branches are allowed (growth rate distribution!). Normally, one-year-old grafts on medium to strong rootstocks are used. If the graft still has no premature shoots or unsuitable lateral shoots, it is best to cut back to a stem height of 15-3/4" to 19-3/4" (40-50cm) with three well formed buds. Of the three buds, two lateral buds should point to the left and right and the uppermost eye should point away from the wall surface. All other buds and shoots in the stem area have to be removed.

The two shoots that develop from the lateral buds are fastened diagonally on the espalier; the upper shoot is trained vertically as the stem elongation and also fastened. However, if a one-year-old graft already has suitable, early shoots that are positioned at the correct height (15-3/4" to 19-3/4" [40-50cm]), then both lateral shoots are fastened diagonally to the framework immediately after being cut back (one-third to one-quarter).

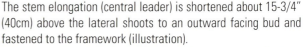

The shoots should not be positioned too flatly in order to ensure appropriate growth.

The stem elongation (central leader) is shortened about 15-3/4" (40cm) above the lateral shoots to an outward facing bud and fastened to the framework (illustration).

When the newly formed lateral shoots have reached an appropriate length, accurate shaping can begin. The necessary lengths depend on whether a four-, six-, or eight-armed Verrier palmette will be trained. If the required lengths for the first branch pair are not attained in the first year, the lateral branches will be cut to one-third/one-quarter of their length in the winter so that a strong growth flush can occur in the following year. The stem elongation is also cut back in winter to approximately 15-3/4" (40cm) above the lateral shoots. The second scaffolding pair is then trained after the lowest tier has developed properly.

When both of the lowest lateral shoots have reached the appropriate length (47" [120cm] with a six-armed Verrier palmette), they are trained horizontally and fastened to the espalier. Afterward, the shoot ends are carefully propped up and fastened to the proper vertical espalier slats. By carefully rotating the shoot ends around on their own axis, breaking them can usually be prevented.

*Older Verrier palmette with
only two branch pairs.*

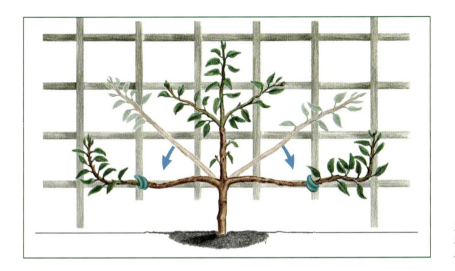

Pruning and shaping tasks in the summer of the first and second years.

Training the first tier often requires two years before the next steps for further development of the crown can be contemplated. The vertically growing shoot ends of the lower tier should already be at least 11-7/8" to 15-3/4" long (30-40cm).

When this length is attained, the stem elongation is again cut back in winter to a length of about 15-3/4" to 19-3/4" (40-50cm). Again, it is important that three well-formed buds are located in the cut area to ensure subsequent growth.

These new shoots are handled in the same way as the shoots from the previous year. Both lateral shoots are trained upward and fastened diagonally, and the stem elongation is attached vertically to the framework slats. Because these next shoot pairs do not have to be as long, they can already be brought into the proper shape as early as August. The shoot ends are again propped up and fastened to the framework.

Occasionally, the lignification rate of the shoots no longer allows the appropriate bending. In this case, incisions can be made on the shoot at the bending point. A shoot break is almost always prevented this way (illustration, pp. 60).

Handle new shoot growths like the shoots from the previous year.

If lateral buds begin to sprout on the lowest branch pair during the second/third year, then the rising shoots are removed.

This stimulates the formation of flower buds and promotes the linear growth of the lower branch pair.

If the vertically positioned shoot ends of the first few arm pairs now reach at least the height of the pruning spot on the stem elongation, the build up of the next arm pair can begin.

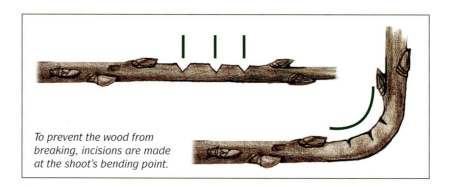

To prevent the wood from breaking, incisions are made at the shoot's bending point.

Three suitable buds must be available at the cut area.

The central leader is cut back in winter to a length of approximately 15-3/4" (40cm), making sure that three suitable buds (two opposing one another for the next branch pair and one bud positioned above and pointing forward for the continuation of the central leader) are available at the pruning spot.

Training the third pair happens in much the same way it did in the previous years. Further pairs could then also be grown using the methods already described.

> If the crown build up is now complete, the last branch pair is cut down to two suitable lateral buds. All other lateral buds on the stem elongation are removed.

Remove all other lateral shoots.

The last branch pair is fastened diagonally, then tied horizontally in August. Later, the shoot ends are fastened vertically. The spacing of branch pairs should be planned out before installing the framework — this will ensure the development of a uniform crown.

Further build-up of the crown in the summer of the third and fourth years.

When the basic palmette design (4, 6, or 8 arms) is completed, it is important to ensure that balance between the individual tiers is maintained well into the future.

The uppermost branch pairs (the central branches) are nurtured considerably more compared to the lower lying branches. While still training, and also during later the maintenance of the crown, make sure that the outer branches are always the longest and tower above the other branch pairs somewhat. They will develop a bit more strongly due to the law of top growth, which prevents the crown form from falling out of balance.

When performing yearly pruning, be sure that the inner branch pairs are cut back more than the outer pairs. In doing so, the cutting plane of the terminal buds on all branch pairs has to angle inwardly.

Another way to support the growth of the outer arms would be to reduce the fruit clusters more on the outside than on the inner branch pairs. A bit less clustering is less restrictive to growth. Furthermore, it is important that the formation of fruiting spurs is observed. Shoots that are positioned too close to one another or growing inwardly should be routinely removed. Fruiting spurs that are in poor condition also have to be routinely removed during winter and summer pruning.

A well-designed Verrier palmette with three branch pairs after the growth flush in spring.

Shoots that are positioned too close to one another should be removed.

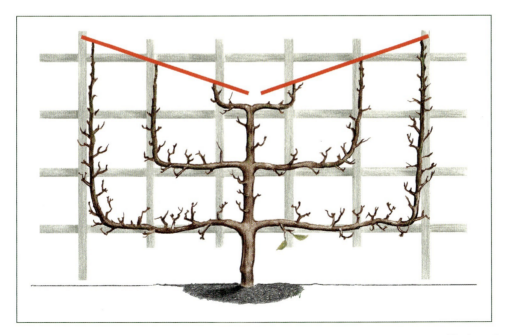

The inner branch pairs must be cut back more.

*The apricot tree's tendency
to form long shoots allows it
to grow on slim fan espaliers.*

One-year-old grafts are best.

Formless Fan Espaliers

Those who don't take as much pleasure in growing more demanding, accurate forms, also have the choice to switch to more irregular espaliers (fan-shaped crowns). The same rules generally apply to cultivation in this case, though, as they do with more advanced forms.

> Fan espaliers are also flat, two-dimensional forms. They are predominantly suitable for various stone fruit varieties, such as peaches, apricots, sweet cherries and sour cherries.

This design is definitely a bit more loosely structured, but the facilitation of uniform growth must also be adhered to with these crowns. The higher sections always grow stronger than lower lying sections in a crown. It is therefore necessary to regularly prune more in the upper crown area to prevent premature bareness and strong growth reduction. To let these crowns "grow out" would soon result in overgrowth and complete suppression of the lower crown section. It is therefore more advantageous to do without direct stem elongation when growing the crown. This way, overgrowth of these crowns can be prevented.

Medium-strength to strongly growing rootstocks are usually used and plant spacing of 13 to 16 feet (4-5m) is necessary to ensure proper development of the fan on both sides.

> This pattern is best for barrier wall heights of up to 6-1/2 feet (2m), but can of course also be trained on any surface, such as house or barn walls.

A stable wire frame is best for the fan espalier. Individual branches of the fan can be attached to the wires with the appropriate spacing for each. Other materials (weaker wood slats, for example) can also be used for the framework construction.

One-year-old grafts, with or without early lateral branching, are best for fan espaliers.

After the earliest possible planting in late winter, the final plant pruning should not occur until the onset of vegetation.

At this point it is clearly visible (more so with stone fruits) which buds are healthy and which are most suitable for pruning. The proper training techniques will be discussed for each of the various fruit varieties.

Stone Fruits

Stone fruits, which are also part of the rose family, include sweet cherries, sour cherries, peaches, nectarines, apricots and the large group of prunes, which includes plums, greengages and mirabelles. Stone fruits have a mostly juicy flesh that encases a hard-shelled pit.

Stone fruits don't have the shelf life of apples or pears, but are great for fresh consumption and processing. Thanks to weaker growing rootstocks, growing smaller stone fruit trees has been made easier, which in turn makes their use in smaller gardens possible.

> Ideally, planting should be carried out at the end of winter (beginning of spring) to prevent any damage from the winter cold (poor enrooting).

Stone fruit varieties are also possible with weaker growing rootstocks.

Formless Fan Espaliers For Peaches and Nectarines

One-year-old peach and nectarine grafts (Heister) already have a number of early lateral shoots, from which two shoots (or four when appropriate) can be chosen for later growing of the fan partitions. The stem height should be at least 15-3/4" (40cm) and not exceed 23-5/8" (60cm).

Under this cut, there should now be suitable lateral shoots on both sides of the stem, which can be grown to create the fan shape. All other lateral shoots must then be removed.

The agreeable arrangement of branches in this apricot fan espalier promises ample exposure to light and thus good fruit development.

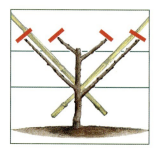

In the beginning, two to four shoots should be left.

The lateral roots selected (two or four) are fastened to the framework at about a 45° angle and cut by one-third of their length.

In the first year, only leaf shoots, which are pruned back again in the spring, emerge from the pruned lateral shoots (future fan partitions).

To achieve an accurate and uniform distribution of the fans, the shoots can be fastened to prepared bamboo rods during the vegetation period.

In addition to leaf shoots, which only have leaf buds in a slim, pointed shape, true fruiting shoots are also forming, which will deliver the first harvest the following year. True fruiting shoots have twin buds (a leaf and a flower bud) or triple buds (a leaf bud with two flower buds) on at least two-thirds of their length; the leaf buds are found in the center.

In the beginning, a maximum of two to four of the available shoots should be left (illustration top left) and it is important that these newly formed shoots receive enough light. They should also continue to be loosely attached to the espalier in a diagonal position. If more abrupt shoots develop in the crown's center, they should be duly removed or, if needed, relocated and fastened to suitable lateral branches (replacement or reserve shoots).

Uniform distribution of shoots is important in the fan-shaped crown.

Beginning in the spring of the tree's third year, the central leaders (fans) will be shortened again by a third to a half at downward-pointing eyes. Naturally, not all shoots can be left in the crown.

> False fruiting shoots in particular (weak shoots that exhibit only flower buds on their entire lengths and, therefore, go bare prematurely) and shoots positioned too abruptly must be entirely removed when pruning at the end of the winter.

True fruiting shoots are shortened to four to eight triple buds. This ensures that the fruits developing here are well-formed and that "true fruiting shoots" can develop from the leaf buds at the same time. The spacing between the fruiting shoots on the end should be at least 7-7/8" (20cm).

Shorten fruiting shoots to 4 – 8 double buds!

In order to ensure proper growth in the lower crown area during later years, pruning should be somewhat shorter here. In contrast, the true fruiting shoots can be left somewhat longer. The higher fruit set achieved by this helps to reduce growth in the top area at the same time. Thus, a certain balance can be accomplished.

Peaches and nectarines bear fruit on one-year-old shoots. If the new shoots are not cut, bare branches can result relatively quickly.

> To maintain young fruiting spurs, yearly pruning is required.

A fully-grown fan espalier must also maintain its shape. This means that worn out and already bare stronger branches have to be replaced by young shoots in order to fully take advantage of the espalier's potential.

Pruning peach trees in less hospitable climates is especially important because the wood of new shoots can never quite mature, making it more susceptible to frost. Due to their distinctive top growth, peach and nectarine trees also tend to go bare from the inside rather quickly. Early shoots, in particular, as well as weaker year-old shoots, die off and the formation of gummosis can also occur.

Also, the ability of vegetative buds (leaf buds) to grow is limited to one to two years, and the tendency of adventitious buds to form rarely exists.

Uniformly distributed branches provide a stable balance within the fan-shaped crown.

> When training fan-shaped peach crowns, it is therefore necessary to severely prune not only the stronger shoots, but also within the entire crown.

The weaker shoots, in particular, should be cut back as short as possible (to one to two eyes), in order to be replaced and to preserve their growing power. For now, they should bear no fruit. In the interest of a longer lifespan and of course quality annual harvests, strong replacement shoots have to develop throughout the crown. Only these shoots can bloom again in the following year and bear fruit. It is advantageous to prune worn out fruiting spurs right after the conclusion of the harvest. This way, the remaining new shoots get more sunlight and nutrients during the rest of the vegetation period and can develop into strong long shoots.

Pruning peach trees is somewhat similar to pruning grape vines, where harvest limbs and new limbs are cut in a similar way. Replacement canes should always remain below the harvest shoots, if possible.

Sweet Cherries

The sweet cherry (P. avium), which comes from the Middle East, was brought to central Europe by the Romans, like many other cultivated plants, and further cultivated there. Because it descends from the wild cherry, its growth is very strong and characterized by its distinct top growth. Sweet cherry varieties develop into relatively large trees on their established rootstocks. Growing a low, small tree, even with pruning and shaping, is unthinkable.

> Another disadvantage is the self-sterility of most varieties, which demand an obligatory pollination partner that lives in the vicinity.

Hybrid cherries must also be treated similarly, but fall somewhere in between the sweet cherry and the sour cherry in their vigor.

Due to the selective breeding of cherry rootstocks that was established in the second half of the twentieth century, a series of weaker growing rootstocks for sweet cherries became available. The Gisela and Weiroot rootstocks (**Gisela 5 and 6** or **Weiroot 53, 72, and 158**) that are used today induce early and ample branching, an early harvest and a relatively even branch outflow, which makes the necessary pruning and shaping easier.

The branch of a peach tree
before and after pruning

Location Requirements

Sweet cherries have no special requirements regarding soil conditions, but cool, moist and heavy soils are more suitable. When using weaker rootstocks in light, sandy, porous soils, additional watering during dry periods is necessary for an appropriate harvest. The sweet cherry tree's resistance to frost is satisfactory (up to -4°F or -20°C), but early flowering can be affected by late frost in some years.

> Most sweet cherries are not self-fruitful and require a pollination partner. This is further complicated by the fact that not every sweet cherry variety can pollinate any other variety.

For a clearer view, varieties were combined in inter-sterility groups, which now make it possible to immediately exclude unfit partners. If only a little space is available, a suitable partner can also be grafted onto the respective crown.

Pruning and Training

The sweet cherry grows strongly and ambitiously by nature. Attempts to create hedge-shaped crown designs or other lower crown forms were usually not successful. New rootstocks eventually produced better results.

Moist soil is more suitable for sweet cherries.

Sweet cherries can also be trained as lower hedge forms using weak growing rootstocks.

Cordons

This growth form is mainly used for producing sweet cherries under glass or foil.

> Slender, column-shaped vertical cordons are grown with a plant spacing of 19-3/4" to 27-1/2" (50-70cm). After a few years on the same cordon length, only fruiting spurs (bouquet shoots) are left.

For the garden lover, though, it is more practical to grow at least two additional lateral branches at the base. Both shoots should be shaped as horizontally as possible and fastened to the framework to slow the top growth of the cordon. The weaker sprouting buds develop later on bouquet shoots and form flower buds relatively quickly.

IMPORTANT:

During the growth period, new shoots that are still in a vegetative phase should have their ends removed several times.

As a result, growth is abated again and again, and ongoing flower bud formation is initiated.

The fully-grown tree should eventually resemble a simple pyramid shape. After attaining the espalier height, the top is diverted to a horizontally positioned lateral shoot. The side growth must also continuously be kept in form during the vegetation period and it helps to cut back several bouquet shoots as well. Shoot elongation is achieved by the growth of the centrally located leaf buds.

Uniform distribution of the main branches is also important with cherry fans.

Fans

To grow sweet cherries in a fan shape, an appropriately large wall surface is required (fence or barrier wall at least 13 to 16 feet wide [4-5m] and about 9-3/4 feet high [3m]). In addition, an appropriate frame (wood slat trellis or wire frame) should be prepared. A one-year-old graft (with or without lateral branching) is used for planting.

A sapling without branching is pruned to about 15-3/4" (40cm) above the ground. If both buds sprout, the shoots can already be fastened to the frame on rods. All other sprouts must be removed.

These two growths constitute the framework for future fans.

In the beginning of the second year, both lateral branches are shortened to about 15-3/4" to 19-3/4" (40-50cm) lengths (4–6 eyes). At the same time, a number of bamboo rods (corresponding to the number of fan partitions) are fastened to the framework and later used to hold the shoots in place. This ensures that they grow outward in a star formation at equal distances.

In order to continue to develop the fan, all shoots trained as central leaders are cut back in the spring of the third year to about 15-3/4" to 19-3/4" (40-50cm) of the previous year's growth. In the summer, the fan will be refilled with new growth. Unnecessary shoots are immediately removed and lateral shoots shortened to about 4" (10cm). If the fan not be completed by the fourth year, the main shoots can be pruned back again. Shoots growing out towards the framework wall or out of the standard form should be removed during spring pruning.

After the development of the crown is complete, it will be necessary to remove older fruiting spurs again or to pinch young lateral shoots in the summer in order to promote the formation of young bouquet shoots.

If the fan grows over the existing framework wall — against expectations — then it is beneficial to cut back the weaker, deviating lateral shoots farther down. Make sure that no tethering materials (strings, wires, etc.) grows in (loosen on time!).

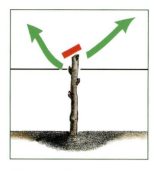

The branchless seedling is pruned to a height of 15-3/4" (40cm).

Left: Pruning and fastening the proper shoots in the summer of the first year. Right: At the beginning of the second year, shoots are pruned back to 19-3/4" in length (50cm).

Sour Cherry (*Prunus cerasus*)

The sour cherry grows markedly weaker than the sweet cherry and is therefore often found in gardens as a shorter shrub tree. The principle form of the sour cherry is the St. Lucie Cherry (P. mahaleb), which exhibits a rather shrub-like growth. Morello cherries have very good branching, but also begin to go bare quite early from the inside out.

The sour cherry is weaker growing than the sweet cherry.

IMPORTANT:

Begin the appropriate pruning measures (heading, thinning out, etc.) relatively early, so that the crown remains airy and balanced.

The fan pattern has proven to be the most suitable for espalier growth.

Sour cherries demand considerably less than sweet cherries and are more adaptable and less susceptible to winter and frost. They also thrive in somewhat harsher high altitudes, but annual rainfall should not be too high due to monilinia (brown rot) infestations. Soil should not be too heavy and not too moist.

Within this very form-rich species, there are self-fruiting and self-sterile varieties. During single plantings, make sure to find out if a fertilization partner is required. The most popular sour cherry variety, the morello cherry, is self-fruiting.

Sour cherries are relatively easy to train on wall frames.

Fans

This espalier form is relatively popular with sour cherries and it is also easier to protect the ripening fruits from birds.

For a sour cherry fan, an 11-1/2 to 14-1/2 feet wide (3.5-4.5m) and at least 6-1/2 feet high (2m) house wall or barrier wall is needed.

Before planting begins, an appropriate wall frame should be built here (similar to frames for peaches or sweet cherries) so that a scaffolding of suitable shoots with equal spacing can be built up here later.

One-year-old grafts with early shoots are usually used for the planting. Two well-located, strong lateral shoots 11-3/4" to 15-3/4" high (30-40cm) are used for the buildup of the first scaffold branches. All other unwanted shoots are completely removed. The two lateral shoots are subsequently cut by a third to a half to one leaf bud pointing upward and then fastened to the framework at about a 45° angle.

At the end of the first growth period, every branch should have produced an appropriate elongation shoot and three to four lateral shoots.

At the beginning of the second year, the shoots left on each side are shortened again by about one-third. The appropriate new shoots are then evenly distributed over the entire surface. If gaps occur during development, another heading cut of the scaffold branches should be done to reach new shoots and integrate them into the build-up of the crown.

If the fan-shaped crown is complete, make sure that old, already worn spurs are replaced by young, new shoots. In early summer, it is important to thin out the young shoots growing on the scaffold branches, where spacing of 4" to 6" (10-15cm) should be maintained. Shorter and medium-length one-year-old shoots normally only have a vegetative bud on the end, through which the growth of the shoot can be resumed. The rest of the buds are usually flowering buds.

Cherry fans can be kept under 6-1/2 feet (2m) with the right rootstock.

These shoots will go bare after the harvest and if they have already become too long, they must be removed or severely cut back (whip shoot formation).

After harvest, shabby branches are cut back to suitable replacement shoots.

Older sour cherry trees often bear fruit only sparsely on the inside. In this case, the four to five-year-old shoots are cut back to young lateral shoots in late summer, after the harvest or in the springtime. Up to one-fourth of the old fruiting spurs can be replaced every year on equally strong-growing trees.

Formless Fan-shaped Crowns of Apricots

In addition to the main fruit varieties of apple and pear, apricots are also frequently found in home gardens. Unfortunately, their life expectancy in our temperate climate zone is much shorter. Therefore, it is especially important to configure the existing location conditions as optimally as possible. Cold, heavy, calcium-deficient soils with groundwater levels that are not too high, as well as fertilizers that are too strong and the use of unsuitable rootstocks, can very strongly affect the development of the tree. Under favorable conditions, like protective house and wall surfaces though, this species, which comes from the dry areas of central Asia, has proven to be very tough.

Initial yields can already be expected after three to four years.

The apricot tree has a shorter lifespan in temperate climates.

Apricots have the shortest winter rest of all fruit varieties, though, and during winter warm spells (Christmas thaw) they can begin producing sap relatively quickly and thus lose their resistance to winter frost.

In cooler climates or outside wine growing areas it is important to use protective stands for planting. Very early flowering also increases risk of late frost, which can be staved off much more easily with wall espaliers. Fan-shaped crowns are relatively well protected by simply covering; with larger trees, however, this course of action is no longer possible.

Apricot growth is particularly strong during the first few years. Long shoots that are few in number but strong-growing are formed with little lateral shoot growth. This rather squarrose growth of the apricot can make training a fan-shaped crown a bit difficult at first. It is important that the designated wall surface is not too small. When using medium-strength growing rootstocks (**St. Julien A, GF 655/2**, for example), it should be at least 26 to 32-3/4 feet (8-10m²). The individual long shoots should then be fastened about 15-3/4" to 19-3/4" (40-50cm) apart from one another and slightly slanted upward on a prepared wire or slatted frame.

Very early flowering increases the risk of a late frost!

The appropriate spacing, combined with light pruning of the long shoots during the first few years, promotes fruiting spur development.

Unsuitable shoots should be consistently removed to always ensure adequate exposure to sunlight within the crown.

The apricot tree bears fruit predominantly on short shoots. Therefore, it is necessary to rejuvenate fruit spurs regularly to maintain the growth potential of the tree. If growth diminishes considerably in later years, the older crown section must be cut back. It is best to perform this kind of rejuvenating pruning after the harvest in summer.

Fruiting spurs have to be regularly rejuvenated.

A one-year-old graft is best for growing an apricot fan. Early shoots can, of course, be included, as long as they are located at the proper height (15-3/4" to 19-3/4" [40-50cm] aboveground). Preferably, shoots should be situated opposite one another and run parallel to the espalier. If such shoots are not available, then the one-year-old shoot is pruned to about 15-3/4" to 19-3/4" (40-50cm) in the spring.

Over the course of the vegetation period, the two most suitable shoots are fastened to the framework at a 45-degree angle. In the spring of the following year (second year), both shoots are pruned again to about 11-3/4" to 15-3/4" (30-40cm) at a bud pointing outward. From the new shoots growing on each lateral branch, three to four stronger shoots with the proper spacing are used for further buildup of the fan espalier. In spring of the third year, a somewhat more severe pruning (heading around one-third of the shoot length) is carried out to promote the development of fruiting spurs (short shoots) and achieve uniform adornment of the entire crown. The fan build-up happens in the same way, even for saplings with early shoots.

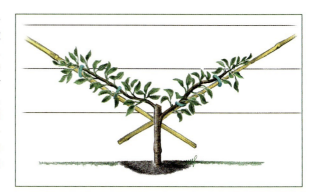

> It goes without saying that uniform growth should be observed even during the vegetation period and the necessary corrections should be made immediately.

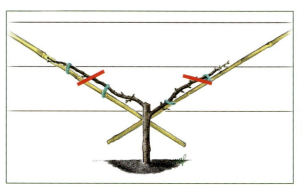

This primarily pertains to steeply growing shoots that don't form correctly. Well-kept crowns usually don't need severe pruning, but bare and unproductive branches should be removed every two to three years in late summer.

The formless fan espalier has proven to be best for apricots. The vulnerability to disease is lower and the fruitfulness of the trees is higher.

Prunes and Plums

Smaller and lower trees were previously very difficult to grow when using rather strong-growing rootstocks — **Brompton and Myrobalans** were in this group as well as Reneklodes and Mirabelles. Through newly developed medium-strength rootstocks (**St. Julien GF 655-2 and Fereley Jaspy**, for example) and weaker growing new breeds (**Pixie, WA x WA**), it is now possible to grow smaller, low-maintenance trees (V-forms, cordon trees, and fan espaliers).

The requirements for using these new rootstocks, however, are fertile soil and the appropriate care.

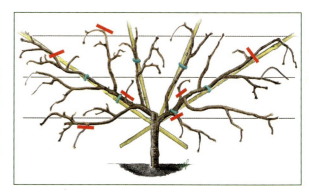

Two shoots are fastened at a 45° angle (top); in the spring of the second year, they are shortened by a 1/3 to 1/4 (middle). In the spring of the third or fourth year, individual main branches can be pruned back once again (bottom).

> Pruning tasks should not occur in the fall or winter, but rather toward the end of spring, in summer or after the harvest.

As a result, the risk of infection by certain diseases (silver leaf or bacterial specks) is greatly reduced.

Fan Espaliers – Training

To ensure an appropriately loose buildup of the fan-shaped crown, the use of medium-strength rootstocks is required along with a wall height of 6-1/2 to 8 feet (2-2.5m) and width of 14-3/4 to 16 feet (4.5-5m). Training the crown is carried out similarly to that of apricots or peaches — a star-shaped crown frame is established that will later sustain uniformly distributed fruiting spurs. An appropriate framework with horizontal wires or wooden slats, on which the frame branches (fan branches) will be fastened, is required for this form. The spacing of the wires, or slats, should be 6" to 9-7/8" (15-25cm) and the bottom wire should be 15-3/4" to 19-3/4" (40-50cm) away from the ground.

Try to build a star-shaped crown!

> Planting prunes can take place from fall to the beginning of spring; pruning can wait until the onset of warmer temperatures.

If the sapling is branchless (one-year-old material is usually used), then it is cut to one bud about 19-3/4" to 23-5/8" (50-60cm) aboveground. Beneath this bud, there must be at least two healthy, opposing buds. After appropriately good growth of all three buds, the upper shoot is cut back in summer since it would be too dominant later. If early shoots are already available, the sapling is cut back to two opposing lateral branches. These two form the first fan partitions of the newly established crown. Other shoots below are completely removed from the beginning.

Left: Pruning the one-year-old graft to the appropriate buds. Right: Main branches are shortened severely early in the second year of cultivation.

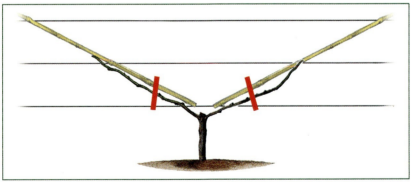

In early summer, two guide rods (bamboo) for stabilizing the new shoots can be fastened to the wires on both sides of the main shoots at a 45° angle. Other new shoots that form during the vegetation period are attached or pinched.

In early spring of the second year, shoots are again cut back to about 11-7/8" to 19-3/4" (30-50cm). Thus, new, strong shoots can develop, which can be used for further buildup of the fan-shaped crown. Depending on space, three to four strong shoots should develop on each side of the fan, which are also secured to rods.

Severely cut back shoots at the beginning of the second year!

> To ensure uniform spurring of the fan-shaped crown, six to eight equally distributed stronger shoots would be necessary.

Additional shoots are handled according to their usability.

In the following years, suitable long shoots are integrated into the existing crown wherever there is enough available space. Otherwise they are duly removed. Punctual pruning procedures in the summer can help short fruiting shoots form.

In the third or fourth year, four to five shoots on each side are chosen and fastened to the framework.

Prunes and plums bloom on one-year-old shoots and on short fruiting spurs; thus, the tendency of branches to go bare increases considerably with age. Later pruning procedures are, therefore, performed so that adequate formation of long shoots as well as short shoots can be encouraged.

It is also important that all shoots growing in the direction of the wall are removed beginning in the spring. Ideally, the space between each strong shoot should be about 4" to 6" (10-15cm). If the spacing is too close, the crown is too thick and has to be countered with appropriate pruning procedures.

Ongoing summer pruning (end removal to four to six leaves) also promotes the consistent formation of new fruiting shoots.

All shoots growing toward the wall must be removed.

More severe pruning can of course also be necessary in later years. It is best to perform these tasks immediately after the harvest or in the following spring.

Developing gaps can then quickly be refilled with new shoots.

Soft Fruits

This very large group also includes different representatives of the ribes genus (currants and gooseberries) and rubus genus (raspberries and blackberries). Due to their shrub-like growth, currants and gooseberries can only be grown for small espaliers (hedges) or for bordering garden beds. Gooseberries and miscellaneous hybrid varieties would also be applicable for property boundaries. Due to their strong growth and entwining ability, grape vines and kiwis, which are also part of this group, are also used for covering large wall surfaces and pergolas.

Soft fruits are great for lower/smaller espaliers!

Currants and Gooseberries

The currants and gooseberries used in our climate also develop well in temperate, cool regions. The heat demands of these berry varieties are considerably lower so that planting in cooler, higher altitudes is also possible. When growing black currants and early-blooming white and red varieties, however, the susceptibility to frost should not be disregarded. Due to the multitude of available varieties, the hobby gardener definitely has the chance to choose a suitable plant. Locations that are known to be susceptible to frost should not be used for planting.

Currants and Gooseberries are usually self-fruitful, but it has been proven time and again that higher yields are only achieved through cross-pollination.

Always plant at least two different varieties!

Therefore, at least two different varieties should always be planted, if space allows.

Currants and gooseberries don't place huge demands on soil depth, but the topsoil should be humid, well-aerated, and nutrient-rich, as well as have ample water capacity. Dry periods are just as damaging to the development of the shrubs as persistent stagnant moisture.

Premature defoliation and permanently small fruit mainly occur in lighter soils and longer, persistent dryness.

Pruning and Trained Growth Patterns

Currants and gooseberries are grown as shrubs, provided that ample space is available. When grafting to suitable rootstocks (Ribes aureum, **gold currant**), several different possible stem heights can be grown. Apart from the forms mentioned, various espalier shapes are found in many gardens today which are primarily suited for somewhat stronger growing varieties.

Left: Gooseberry cordon trees ease pruning and harvesting work. Right: Two branch hedge – training each axis is carried out on the espalier.

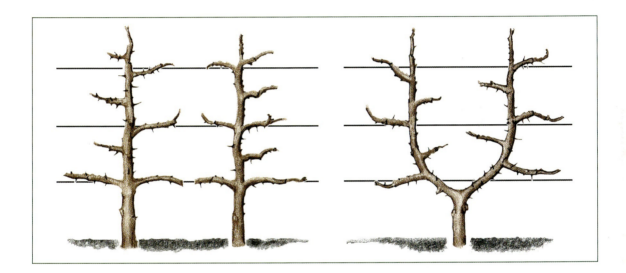

Several designs are possible for espalier growth, such as slender spindles, two or three branch hedges, or fan espaliers. These growth patterns require a suitable wire frame (possibly with double wire bracing) or a suitable wall frame for fan-shaped growth. The very slender, vertical cordon trees of currants and gooseberries are particularly suitable for smaller gardens.

Planting currants and gooseberries can take place from fall until early spring. Depending on the growth pattern, plant spacing ranges from at least 19-3/4" to 39-3/8" (50-100cm). To ensure appropriate growth, pruning should be performed every fall.

> Shoots that are not needed for further growth are removed immediately, while those intended for the elongation of the central axis are cut back by about a third to a half to promote a strong growth flush.

A very good fruit set on a currant cordon.

A small free-standing espalier can also be furnished relatively easily with protective bird netting.

When growing this form, the development of a base stem with a length of 4" to 11-7/8" (10-30cm) has proven to be advantageous.

The lowest positioned scaffold branches are fastened to the lowest frame wire as soon as they have reached an appropriate length, and the designated stem elongation is pinched about 7-7/8" to 15-3/4" (20-40cm) above the lateral shoots. This is done in a similar way the following year with the lateral shoots developing here. All one-year-old shoots that are not needed are routinely removed.

> To ensure a uniform harvest in later years, regular pruning of fruiting spurs must be carried out beginning in the third or fourth year of cultivation.

Only then is an ample reformation of fruiting spurs assured. Summer and winter pruning should complement one another.

Because their fruiting spurs maintain a relatively short length, currant and gooseberry cordons (vertical cordons) are easier to care for and harvest.

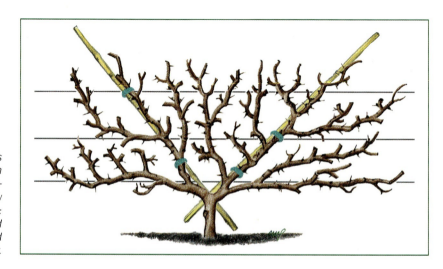

Gooseberry fan espalier – it's important to have uniform distribution of the main branches. The fruiting spurs grow like they do on cordon trees: the lateral shoots are pinched in the summer and shortened again at the end of winter.

If they are not trained onto an espalier, they definitely require support since the central axis doesn't develop as strongly. Strong bamboo rods (6 to 6-1/2" feet long or 1.8-2m) have proven useful for this.

Bamboo rods make great supports.

After planting, the strongest shoot (future lead shoot) is cut back by up to a half of the new growth. Sprouts and buds are removed from the area of the future stem and the rest of the shoots are cut back to two eyes.

In the summer of the first year, new shoots that are too long should be shortened to four to six leaves and the central leader should be fastened to the support.

In early spring of the second year, before the growth flush, lateral shoots are again shortened to one to two eyes in order to encourage the development of strong fruiting branches. The central leader is repeatedly cut back. As soon as the desired height is reached (6 feet [1.8m] on espaliers), the previous year's growth is cut back to one bud to halt growth.

Currant and gooseberry fans can also be very decorative. These forms can be grown on walls, lower barrier walls or fences, where they receive sufficient light.

They should not be exposed to continuous direct sunlight (south-facing) though.

To save time growing fan espaliers, primarily with currants, a suitable two-year-old shrub that already has proper lateral shoots can be used. These shoots (3 – 5) are dispersed according to available space, cut back and fastened to the framework (illustration below). All remaining shoots have to be removed.

To save time, plant a two-year-old old shrub.

The development of the fan's scaffold branches generally takes a few years. The dominant scaffold branches are handled like those of cordon trees, which emanate from a single point in a star shape.

During the vegetation period (main growth period), new green shoots on branches should be shortened to four to six leaves, while some of the shoots can be cut back to one

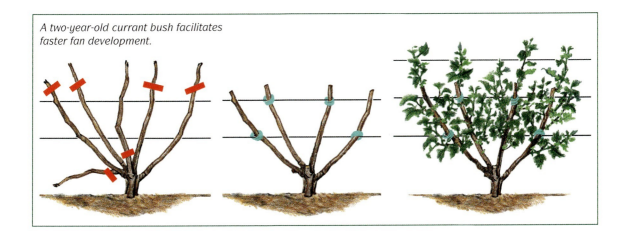

A two-year-old currant bush facilitates faster fan development.

Currant fans with three main branches.

to two eyes in winter in order to promote the formation of short shoots. If such fan espaliers are to be trained on a wall, remove at least some of the rear-facing sprouts (for better circulation).

Maintenance Procedures

> Because the ribes varieties enroot somewhat flatter, loosening the soil too deeply around the root crown should not occur.

Usually, a simple loosening at the surface combined with moderate mulch covering is enough to stop or suppress weed growth. This also minimizes water loss in the soil. Additional watering (possibly drip irrigation) is essential on light, sandy soils.

Only chloride-free fertilizers should be used since currants and gooseberries are sensitive to chloride. Over the course of the vegetation period, appropriate pest control methods are performed, if necessary. Gall mites appear frequently on currant trees and can lead to a thickening of buds. These can be removed mechanically. After the growth flush, damage to leaves can also occur — this must be systematically treated with pesticides.

When discussing gooseberries, American gooseberry blight must be mentioned. It can be combated mechanically (cutting off infested shoot ends) and chemically, with a suitable sulfur-based agent. For the hobby gardener, using less vulnerable varieties (Invicta or Rolanda, for example) is recommended. Rolanda, in particular, is very resistant to American gooseberry blight.

Blackberries

Wild blackberries (rubus fruticosus and other varieties) are normally strong-growing, climbing half-shrubs from the rose family (rosaceae).

> The tendrils, which are generally heavily studded with prickles, can already bear fruit in the second year, but then mostly die off.

Today there are many prickle-free varieties.

Today there are a large number of prickle-free varieties (thrornless evergreen, for example) that also have equally good yields.

There are also a series of rubus hybrids on the market (Loganberries and Tayberries, for example) that have fewer prickles, which makes work considerably easier. Nevertheless, proper hand protection is always advised.

In English-speaking countries, where this berry variety is quite important, over two hundred varieties are known. Berries can range from puce to black-colored and egg-shaped to hemispheric. In our part of the world, though, very little cultivation experience exists.

Location Demands

The blackberry does not place any special demands on soils, but satisfactory harvests are only achieved in appropriately humic soils with sufficient moisture. Timely watering during fruit ripening, especially in dry times, can greatly improve the quality of the fruits. Working the soil too deeply is also rather detrimental here. Mulch (covering with organic material) has proven to be the most beneficial. The planting area can be prepared by loosening the soil, introducing organic substances and incorporating a basic fertilizer for the planting.

> Early spring planting is best since drought damage can occur after poor enrooting in the fall.

It is important to use strong, healthy plants in order to ensure quick growth and strong, early development.

It's also important to have the correct plant spacing. When planting in rows or along fencing, strong-growing varieties should be spaced 6-1/2 to 8 feet (2-2.5m) apart, and weaker-growing varieties 3 to 5 feet (1-1.5m). The space between rows should not be less than 6-1/2 feet (2m) to ensure sufficient exposure to sunlight. A stable frame (wire frame, stable fence, etc.) is essential for suitable cultivation management. A wire frame (zinc coated material 1/8" or 2.5-2.8mm) should have at least three wires (four are better) and the frame height should not be much more than 6 to 6-1/2 feet (1.8-2m).

Blackberries also make beautiful espaliers.

Pruning and Training Methods

With blackberries and other hybrids, winter pruning (early spring pruning) and summer pruning (lopping) differ from one another.

At the end of winter, all worn, two-year-old tendrils are cut just above the ground and removed. From the newly formed tendrils, four to six strong shoots per plant are kept and, after the removal of old tendrils, interlaced on the wire frame (depending on trained growth method).

Use strong and healthy plants!

During summer pruning, overlooked axle shoots are cut back to one to two eyes and long or dead shoot ends are shortened.

Between about mid-July and the beginning of August, young, newly-formed shoots on tendrils are removed two or three times.

Shortly before the lateral shoots begin to lignify on the new shoots, they are eventually cut back to two to three leaves to ensure the maturity of the buds.

At the same time, weaker ground shoots can also be removed; but for any developing frost damages, it is better to leave a certain reserve.

Generally, there are three trained growth systems:
■ Double Wire System
On this system, vertical stakes are used with a short crossbeam 6" to 7-7/8" (15-20cm) and set at an appropriate distance. After the growth flush of plants, newly formed tendrils are trained (threaded) on one side of the wire frame.

After the preparatory pruning measures already described, these tendrils develop fruiting shoots in the second year. The newly advancing shoots in the second year are formed on the other (free) side, whereby a biennial rhythm is developed. To ease pruning and harvesting tasks, fruit bearing tendrils and new shoots are separated.

With this method, new shoots are mostly trained straight up, which can suppress the formation of axle shoots. After the harvest, as soon as the fruit bearing shoots have been removed from the left and right, new shoots develop on the side and are fastened to the wire frame.

In a double wire system, shoots can be easily threaded.

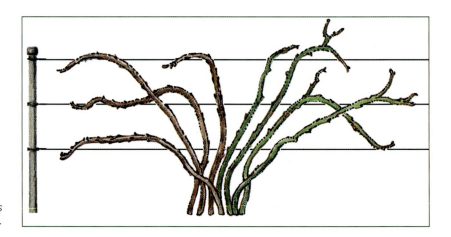

Espalier with shoots divided by age.

Espalier with upright, young shoots in the middle. The fruiting shoots are found on the sides.

■ Palmetto

With this trained growth pattern too, the old tendrils of one year are fastened to one side and the following years' tendrils to the other side. After harvesting the fruits, worn fruiting shoots are removed and space is made for the new shoots for the following year.

> The advantage of this system is that the tendrils only have to be fastened one time, which means time spent on maintenance is kept rather low.

Since young shoots grow on top of one another, the transmission of fungal diseases from the two-year-old tendrils is also limited.

A property boundary is formed with the help of a blackberry hedge.

■ Fan

In this case, fruit bearing tendrils are divided in the row and fastened more or less vertically on the wire framework. Thus, some free space remains in the middle for new tendrils, which are immediately fastened to the frame or on the highest wire when they are too long. Alternating the tendrils is carried out as already described on the front area.

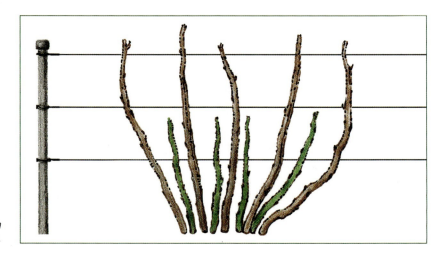

New tendrils alternate with the fruit bearing shoots.

Kiwi (Actinidia deliciosa)

The Chinese gooseberry, as it is also called, is a very strong-growing, climbing plant, which is already widespread in warmer, moderate, and non-frost-prone regions of Europe.

They can also be planted in most domestic wine regions, but their long, soft new shoots are very sensitive to frost.

The fruits can also be damaged by early frost in fall and freeze.

Kiwi plants have relatively large, soft, heart-shaped leaves, which also exhibit light fuzz. The new shoots have a reddish color, which later disappears. Flowers reveal a yellowish color. Male flowers have only stamens, while female flowers feature several styles with stigmas in addition to stamens (illustration p. 85, left).

Kiwis have large leaves with light fuzz.

Varieties like A. chinensis are only conditionally suitable for planting outdoors. For hobby gardeners with perhaps not completely optimal climate conditions, varieties like A. arguta and A. kolomikta are more suitable. Both varieties are frost resistant, exhibit a weaker, more shrub-like growth by nature, and are, therefore, very well suited for growing in a free fan-shaped form.

A reasonably stable fence often suffices as the framework for this kind of hedge.

In Europe today, there are already more than a dozen known varieties of this popular species. The following list provides a small outline.

Female flower with protruding style crown and male flower with developed stamens (left). Relatively frost resistant kiwi varieties are also widespread in Europe (right).

Small Fruit Kiwi Varieties

Variety	Color	Taste	Fruit Size/weight	Fruit shape	Yield
Kiwino	light green	sweet, aromatic	0.35-0.63 oz. (10-18g)	flat, cylindrical	high
Ambrosia	light green	sweet, aromatic	0.35-0.49 oz. (10-14g)	flat, cylindrical	high
Weiki	green-rosy red	sweet, aromatic	0.14-0.35 oz. (4-10g)	longish-roundish	very high
Polygama	green	sweet, peel sour	0.18-0.35 oz. (5-10g)	spherical	high
Geneva verte	light green	sweet, peel sour	0.14-0.21 oz. (4-6g)	spherical	very high
Kiwai rouge	rust red	sour, plain aroma	0.14-0.21 oz. (4-6g)	longish-round	very high

Since the varieties are in large part diocious, planting pollinating varieties (Nostino, for example) is beneficial and necessary. Despite good fruitfulness, its characteristic biennial fruiting is usually difficult to eliminate.

Large fruit kiwi varieties are all diocious, which means they always require a pollination partner. It is important that these plants are located next to a female partner [ratio ca. 1:7 (♀)].

Male kiwi plants are grown similarly to the female blooming plants and can also be severely cut back after blossoming to save space.

Of the large-fruit kiwi varieties "Hayward" (the most important), "Abhart," "Monty," "Bruno," "Staiello," and "Allison" are predominantly used. The male variety "Matua" has proven to be the best pollinator.

Training and Pruning

Due to growth behavior, two trained growth designs are suitable:

■ Espalier

Planting can take place between late fall and spring and spacing of large fruit varieties should be 10 to 13 feet (3-4m). Spacing of smaller kiwi varieties can be reduced by half due to weaker growth.

The framework must be stable (two to three stronger stakes) and should be strung with at least three wires at intervals of 23-1/2" to 27-1/2" (60-70cm), 51" to 55" (130-140cm), and 74-7/8" to 78-3/4" (190-200cm), each measured from the ground. For better cultivation, a strong bamboo rod should also be provided next to each plant, attached vertically on the wires.

After planting, prune back to 11-7/8" to 15-3/4" (30-40cm) to ensure a strong growth flush.

> If growing an accurate espalier is planned, it is necessary to train a lead shoot as vertically as possible on the existing bamboo rod in the first and second growth periods.

Strong lateral shoots should emerge from the stem on the right and left; unnecessary shoots have to be removed immediately. When the stem has grown out over the last wire and the lateral shoots have reached the appropriate length (> 3' or 1m long), it is necessary to pinch (end removal). Thus, lateral growth is stimulated and encouraged.

The framework should be stable and strung with three wires.

In southern Europe pergola forms are used for kiwi production.

The later developing shoots from the buds of the lateral shoots, are shortened again in midsummer to five leaves (often several times), in order to promote a base formation of fruiting spurs. Competitive shoots should always be completely removed during the course of such pruning measures. The harvest is usually established by the third year.

With the more simple growth of a fan-shaped crown, a number of the shoots emanating above the root crown (growing spot) are trained in a fan form on the prepared framework. Further fastening is usually not necessary later since the tendriled shoots find sufficient hold to the wire frame.

After the harvesting phase, it is best to perform the first pruning tasks in the beginning of spring. In doing so, worn out fruiting branches are exchanged for young fruiting shoots and at the same time other necessary new shoots are fastened to the espalier. In order to maintain a sufficient amount of new shoots for the fruiting shoots, particularly in the base area, fruit bearing branches should also be shortened during the vegetation period to four to six behind the last fruit.

The newly developing growth here is later shortened again to one to two eyes. Through this ongoing interruption of the sap flow, the buds closest the base, in particular, are stimulated and balding of branches is prevented.

With older plants, part of the older fruiting branches (three to four year cycle) can be cut back to adventitious buds in order to achieve new growth near the base.

■ Pergola

This form of growth is very well-suited for actinidias and double-breasted pergolas have proven to be very usable, provided there is enough space. The height of the frame should not exceed 6-1/2 feet (2m) so that later pruning and harvesting tasks are not complicated.

Kiwi plants are trained up with a stem for now. This stem, together with two horizontally trained lead shoots growing in opposite directions, forms the base frame. Developing lateral shoots of the two lead shoots will be used to cover the pergola later and will eventually form the foundation for fruit bearing branches.

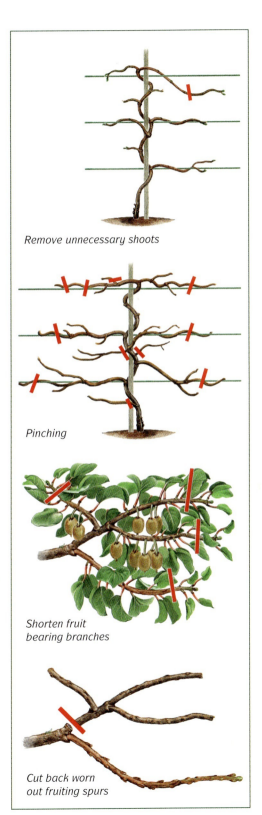

Remove unnecessary shoots

Pinching

Shorten fruit bearing branches

Cut back worn out fruiting spurs

Shoots located further down on the stem (provided there are any left) can still be trained like free-standing fan-shaped formations.

> Regular pruning should also be performed with a pergola growth. This ensures sufficient branching of the otherwise meter-long growing shoots and guarantees uniform fruitfulness.

The pruning and rejuvenation cycle can be performed in a similar way, as previously explained. Consistent thinning out of the pergola crown is important in order to ensure that fruiting spurs receive ample exposure to light and fruit bearing branches are evenly distributed.

Maintenance Procedures

The soil should always be kept free of competing weeds in the stem area since kiwi plants react sensitively to water and nutrient competition. Covering the area with different organic materials has proven to be very beneficial.

Actinidias are quite resistant to diseases and pests. Nevertheless, pests from other know fruit varieties colonizing kiwi plants can not be ruled out. Aphids, in particular, can cause shoot swelling and leaf deformation as well as growth depressions. Pesticides are then necessary here.

Scale insects can also cause damage to hairy leaves, shoots and fruits through their constant feeding. Mechanical and chemical actions could collectively help combat them. Fungal diseases, particularly botrytis and verticillium wilt, can also appear.

Kiwis are quite resistant to diseases and pests.

The fruit bearing branches are evenly distributed here.

Such infestations can be reduced by working cautiously and avoiding injuries.

In our part of the world, diseases can also occasionally appear on the growing spot. Sometimes these are malignant tree growths, which can also lead to tree bark loss. The interrupted sap flow can eventually lead to the death of the entire plant. The cause of these changes, however, is not yet completely clear (possibly frost exposure), but their appearance is very similar to collar rot on apple trees.

Diseases are more frequent on the growing spot.

Grapevines

Grapes are strong-growing, deciduous climbing plants, which are extremely adaptable and found in many regions of the world. Purpose-grown varieties are almost exclusively from the species vitis vinifera. In cooler climates, these heirloom grapes prosper better on protected, sunlit house or barrier walls. More robust varieties, though, are very popular as espalier plants.

This old vine in Sicily was trained upward for the construction of a pergola on a balcony.

Originally, grapes grew wild on forest trees. When no adequate supports or climbing aids exist, they grow evenly along the ground.

Grapevines have to be pruned regularly for sustainable use otherwise they become a copse of young and dead tendrils that only produce a small quantity of substandard grapes.

A series of pruning methods are employed for training and shaping.

The goal of this work is to form a framework base that ensures yearly growth of new shoots and a good harvest in the following years.

Pruning grapevines is best performed at the end of winter. At this time, fresh cutting spots "bleed" very little; this means very little sap is squeezed out of cut limbs and the plants are not unnecessarily weakened by it.

The varieties of the vitis vinifera species used today are generally grafted to suitable rootstocks, which are resistant to phylloxera. Even native grape varieties grown on their own roots (so-called direct carriers) are not affected. Today, crossbreeds of native varieties with American rootstock grapes exist that are also resistant to some fungal diseases and therefore rarely require any pesticides. In our not-so-favorably warm climes, grape vines are primarily found on protective, warmer house walls, where the grapes are predominantly used for fresh consumption.

Planting (slightly angled toward the framework)

Planting and Care

The best time to plant is April/May, but container goods can also be planted well into the summer. The planting pit for grape vines should not be measured to small (up to a square yard [1m²] according to need and necessity, and at least 19-3/4" [50cm] deep). The subsoil should also be thoroughly loosened to ease later enrooting. If several plants are to be planted in a row, spacing of 5 to 6-1/2 feet or 1.5-2m (depending on the trained growth form) should be maintained.

The demands on the soil are quite low. Only significantly waterlogged earth is not tolerated. Soil should be loose and porous, but not too dry and a bit calciferous.

> Ideally, the enrooted grapevine is somewhat angled toward the prepared frame, about 11-7/8" to 15-3/4" (30-40cm) away from the wall. With grafted grape vines, it is important to remember that the growing spot not be buried.

Adequate watering after planting should not be forgotten. Mulch covering can also be used with grapevines, to help protect the planting area. If the plants are located in the rain shadow of a house wall, it is important to water regularly to prevent drought damage of the young plants. Good compost or well-decomposed horse manure makes the best fertilizer.

Lopping plays an important role!

Lopping during the vegetation period plays an important role when training an espalier. This especially applies to the foliage of grapevines.

IMPORTANT:

The uniform distribution and timely fastening of new shoots, the removal of unwanted sprouts in the stem, and the pruning of non-fruiting shoots, which are not needed for the build-up of the structure, should be carried out.

Removing the ends of axle shoots in late summer can contribute to improved lignification of the grapevine. Simply picking grapes at the point of ripeness can considerably improve the outer and inner quality of the harvested material.

A certain degree of plant protection is also required with grape vine espaliers; fungal diseases, in particular, require a lot of attention. In recent years, however, resistant varieties are increasingly planted, which helps to minimize the use of various agents. The most common fungal diseases are powdery mildew, downey mildew, pseudopezicula tracheiphila, and botrytis cinerea. The main animal pests are mites, which cause great damage. Bird protection should also be considered and in some years wasp control.

> Plant protection is also necessary for grapevine espaliers!

Grapevines also entwine themselves up on simple mesh grids made of metal.

Espalier Forms

Grapevine espaliers can grow on more demanding designs (vertical or horizontal cordons, U-shapes) as well as in a more natural fan-shaped form. However, before the actual training can begin, the plant should be well rooted and also already possess an appropriate shoot (or several).

> For this reason, young grapevines are cut back to two to three buds after planting; this is repeated again the next year until the shoots have attained the proper strength and the necessary growth potential.

Do not cut directly
above the eye!

In contrast to the pruning techniques of pome fruits, grapevines are not cut just above an eye. Instead, a piece about 3/8" to 3/4" long (1-2cm) is left above the buds, which prevents the buds from drying out prematurely and promotes growth. New branch series should always be pruned whenever the underlying series has become strong and completely developed.

In order to ensure a maturing of the vine stock and grapes, early or moderately early ripening varieties are definitely preferred.

> With grapevines, a supporting framework for the old growth (stem, cordon or arches) is always needed for the buildup of different forms.

To ensure a certain spacing to the ground surface, a stem 15-3/4" to 19-3/4" or longer (40-50cm) should always be intended. Vertical and horizontal cordons, different arch forms or simple fan-shaped espaliers are suitable trained growth forms.

The vertical cordon (single-arm) is more suitable for weak-growing varieties because they are more tolerant when pruning canes.

When the stem elongates, a stronger shoot is fastened vertically to the framework and set back above the sixth to the eighth eye during winter pruning. From the forming shoots, the uppermost shoot is fastened vertically to the framework and the rest are fastened on the side for now. In the following winter pruning, the central leader is again cut above the sixth to eighth eye, while the lateral shoots are cut back to canes (two eyes). This is repeated until the cordon length has reached the top of the espalier.

The vertical cordon is good
for weak-growing varieties.

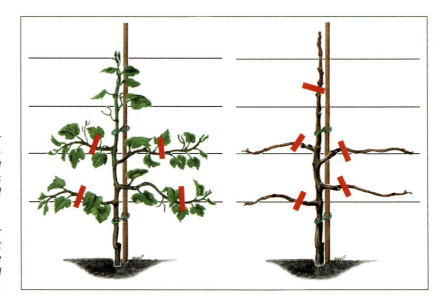

Left: First year summer (after planting) – The uppermost shoot is trained vertically, the axle shoots are fastened to the side and the ends are removed.

Right: Second year winter pruning – The stem is cut back to two-thirds and the lateral shoots are shortened to canes (one to two buds).

When training this vertical cordon, the fruit bearing branch series are arranged about 9-7/8″ to 11-7/8″ (25-30cm) above one another on each side. If several vine stocks are planted next to one another, spacing of at least 3 to 5 feet (1.0-1.5m) should be maintained. This slim trained growth form can be used on narrower house or barrier walls.

Summer pruning is similar with all forms that are cut on canes. New shoots are cut above the seventh or eighth eye in August so that the remaining eyes (buds) can mature appropriately. Only two shoots are preserved on each cane. These, and possibly the lateral shoots growing on the elongation shoot, later have their ends removed two to three leaves above the uppermost fruit.

It is best to cut back other shoots of the second array to one to two eyes.

While two eyes (hence two shoots) per cane are left on fully-grown grapevines in the beginning, it is more beneficial in later years to let more summer shoots grow on each cane. The weaker shoots are shortened to two to three leaves. For a better distribution, the summer shoots can be carefully trained downward, fastened to the framework and then shortened to two leaves above the highest fruit. In the following year the cane pruning is repeated.

In certain circumstances it can also be necessary to reduce the number of grapes per plant.

New shoots have their ends removed above the seventh and eighth eye!

Shoots not bearing fruit are cut back to four to six leaves!

Summer (second year): The highest shoot is elongated again and fastened; upon fruiting, lateral shoots are shortened to two leaves above the highest grape, otherwise they are cut back to four to five leaves.

> **RULE OF THUMB:**
>
> For each 11-7/8" (30cm) of stem length, 17-1/2 ounces (500g) of grapes are grown. Later, the complete yield is four to six grape clusters per stem.

Especially well suited for growing around windows!

It demands a bit more attention to grow two-armed or multiple-armed vertical cordons per vine, where at least three feet (1m) spacing is maintained between vertical stems. If growing two cordon arms above the stem, for example, two tendrils are trained to both sides, first horizontally and then, spaced three feet (1m) apart from one another, vertically upward.

Pruning and further training is carried as already described. This form is especially suitable for growing around doors and windows.

U-form with two vertical cordons (window framing)

Horizontal Grapevine Cordons

These cordons are frequently used with lower boundary walls. With this form, a 7-7/8" to 11-7/8" (20-30cm) stem is grown and then branching of the main limbs can begin. It can be trained with one or two arms, depending on how the available space is configured. It is easiest to grow the two-armed form so that the already existing main shoot is trained horizontally at first. This is also how a single-arm cordon is formed. The end is removed from this part a bit later, 15-3/4 to 23-3/4" (40-60cm) after the bending spot.

By doing this, the buds nearest to the bending spot are stimulated to grow.

The strongest, most suitable shoot is later carefully bent again to form the second cordon. Further pruning measures correspond to those of the vertical cordon.

Palmettes
A simple palmette form with nearly horizontal lateral branches also requires an appropriate espalier frame. The stem height for this form should be about 15-3/4" to 23-3/4" (40-60cm) or longer for high espaliers and the cultivation of the central leader occurs in a similar way to the vertical cordon. Pruning the lateral tendrils (branch series) is similar to pome fruit pruning; they are also cut back to three buds and the highest bud is used for the elongation of the central leader and the two side buds are used for the formation of tiers. The spacing between tiers should be about 19-3/4" to 23-3/4" (50-60cm). Several levels can be constructed, depending on the size of the available surface space.

Prune the lateral tendrils to three buds!

A very similar trained growth form, which is only used for lower espaliers (up to 5 feet/1.5m) since only two or three shallow arches are grown, is the so-called **shallow arch design**. In the first few years, the strongest possible shoot is trained to the highest wire of the frame. To make this easier, the shoot can be regularly fastened to a suitable rod that is also attached to the framework. The ends of sprouting eyes are consistently removed in the summer of the first year to two to three leaves. In the second year, two or four suitable, strong shoots (one or two on each side) are left and the ends are removed at a later time. The shoot elongation is cut off just above the wire.

Leave two to four strong shoots in the second year!

At the beginning of the third year, the two (or four) selected shoots are fastened along the top and bottom wires and shortened to ten to twelve eyes.

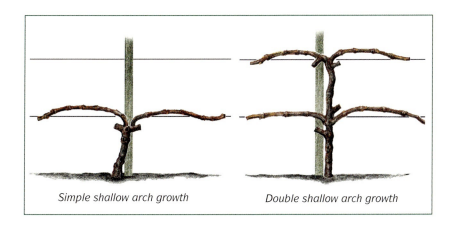

Simple shallow arch growth   *Double shallow arch growth*

In order to get replacement shoots again the following year, additional shoots near the four branches must be cut back to two to three eyes (replacement canes!).

All other shoots are broken off or pinched.

In the spring of the following years, worn out fruiting spurs are removed. Replacement shoots form and are fastened. Pruning for suitable replacement canes is most important here.

Fans

You are not bound to any specific shape with this trained growth form. In fact, the size and shape of the surface area determines the potential dispersion. Winter and summer pruning should complement one another. The distribution of fruiting spurs relies on the already described pruning rotation of fruit-bearing grapes and canes.

IMPORTANT:

To fully take advantage of available space, make sure there is a uniform distribution of later developing "old growth" during build-up.

Pergolas

Pergolas require an appropriately stable frame on which the shoots of the vine stock are grown and attached.

Entryways should run as close to a north-south direction as possible, in order to ensure appropriate exposure to sunlight.

Vertically trained cordons are great for pergolas!

Vertically trained cordons have proven to be very useful for the creation (or development) of these pergolas. It is important that uniform coverage is attained and also maintained by the appropriate pruning rotation and rejuvenation. Grapevines bear fruit on shoots that have emerged from one-year-old growth. Summer shoots, which are formed on older growth sections (older than three years), generally don't develop inflorescence and remain fruitless. The pruning length of the fruit bearing spurs varies and depends on the fruitfulness of each variety and of course on the growing strength of each plant. Pruning grapevines — which is again advised — is performed about 1/2" (1.5cm) above the eye (bud) since cutting too close results in the bud drying out easily and dying.

Quince (Cydonia oblonga L.)

The quince, which originates from southwestern Asia and is now found in southern Europe, should be in every fruit lover's garden. This rather tree-like growing fruit variety is also quite hardy in our part of the world, but usually does not make it through biting frosts without some damage.

The location demands of the quince are rather low. Loose, humus-rich and not-too-heavy soils with low calcium content can greatly improve the development of the plants.

In contrast to the apple or the pear, the quince tree is rather small and is therefore used as a weak-growing rootstock for pears where possible (no affinity problems). Even the quince heirloom varieties in use today are grafted to native rootstocks (**Quince A, C**).

The pannose, yellow- to ocher-colored fruits, also need sufficient fall warmth for proper ripening; this is when they develop their characteristic quince aroma. In the past they were placed in closets and chests for their fragrance, which is known to have a certain effect against moths and cockroaches. In central Europe the fruits usually don't ripen completely and can therefore not be eaten raw. However, they are processed into delectable jellies, marmalades and stewed fruits. When placed on wooden grates in a dark, cool room, the fruits keep for at least one to two months after harvest.

> Young plants are considerably more susceptible to frost. Thus, it is advantageous to plant quince in the spring.

When using one-year-old grafts, pruning back five to six eyes above the growing spot is carried out after planting. With two-year-old plants, three to four suitable scaffold branches are chosen and the remaining shoots removed for now. These selected shoots then form the basic structure for the later trained fan espalier. These shoots are shortened by about one-third for now, but care should be taken that the cutting spots are made in a plane (sap balance!).

In the following years too, it will necessary to shorten these main branch elongations time and again in order to ensure appropriate growth.

After the completion of the crown build-up, the appropriate corrections are made, such as removing branches growing from the inside or removing worn fruiting spurs — quinces fruit on fruiting spurs and short shoots that develop on the previous year's long shoots.

Completely ripe quinces before the harvest (top). Quinces are also quite hardy in our part of the world (bottom).

> Not all one-year-old long shoots and newly created lateral shoots should be shortened, since the flower buds formed on the ends would be lost.

Quinces can also be trained as pyramids

To reduce the crown height, the appropriate lower lateral branches are cut back. With any future rejuvenation that may be necessary, old growth can definitely be cut back more severely as well.

Quinces can, of course, be trained as pyramid crowns too, but a support is required for the first few years. Such a crown construction can be completed after about five to six years.

Quinces frequently tend to form stump shoots. If this kind of growth forms on the base of the trunk, they have to be removed as quickly as possible. Shoots in the stem area (underneath the crown) also need to be cut or broken off as early as possible.

Quinces are self-fruitful; therefore it is not necessary to plant two different varieties together. They should always have the best (most protective) spot in the garden.

*Blooming medlar trained
as a melee stem*

Medlar (Mespilus germanica)

The medlar is rarely encountered in the garden, but it can definitely be grown into an attractive ornamental tree. Medlars are normally cultivated as meter or half-standard trees. They are, like the quince, also self-fruitful. The fruits feature a brown color and in the fall they have to ripen a bit post-harvest before they can be processed or eaten. A light frost can accelerate this post-harvest ripening somewhat.

Individual varieties exhibit slightly varying growth; for example, "Nottingham" and "Royal" grow quite upright while the variety "Dutch", in contrast, looks more like a weeping willow.

The natural, but rather shrub-like medlars love loose, moist soils, and locations that are not always optimally sunny are sufficient. The varieties are also grafted to pears, quinces or hawthorn.

> In the first few years after planting, the plants need support in the form of a stake or framework, and pruning is best carried out in winter.

*Well formed medlar fruit
in fall before harvest*

Similar to the quince, the designated main branches are shortened by about one-third to outward pointing buds. Weaker shoots are cut back to one to two eyes or completely removed. After completion of the crown structure, only smaller pruning cuts (thinning out, shaping) are necessary. With a fan-shaped growth, the growth behavior of each individual variety (upright or hanging) should be considered.

Fig (Ficus carica)

Recently, the fig tree has also found its way into gardens and onto patios, although it is actually native to sub-tropical and tropical regions.

> A complete ripening of the fruits in outdoor areas, however, can only be expected in mild wine-growing climates or with appropriate frost protection in winter.

The fig varieties used in our region also bear fruit without pollination (parthenocarpy) and therefore can be easily grown in buckets that protect them from winter frost.

If the plants are cultivated outdoors, care should be taken to ensure that the location is sunny and above all protected.

In gardens, the fig is primarily grown as a low bush (6-1/2 to 10 feet or 2-3m). Because it is relatively easy to train, fan-shaped crowns on suitable house or barrier walls are easy to grow. Reproduction is usually carried out by scions, but its willingness to take root often varies greatly. It is more advantageous to obtain suitable materials in a tree nursery. This can be a bare-rooted graft or a container plant. The best time to plant is in the spring, and the soil should be reasonably loose, humus-rich and retain water well.

Figs are well suited for fan-shaped crowns.

> Due to their relatively large leaves, figs have a higher demand for water in the summer, but the substrata can also not dry out completely in the winter (not less than 25–30%).

Bushes are grown with very short stems or without. Fan-shaped crowns, in contrast, should always have a short stem 11-7/8″ to 19-3/4″ (30-50cm). It is also important to care for root unification, if the fan-shaped crown should maintain a moderate size. Plants grown in a pot or bowl already have a certain limitation to later growth.

Fig trees, here with fruits, grow well in pots (left). Figs have large leaves, thereby requiring regular watering in the summer (right).

Under good conditions and without limitations to root growth, a fig crown can certainly become oversized, but produce very little fruit.

Pruning a fig plant should take place in February/March, before the new growth flush, in order to prevent a milky sap discharge that is too strong. This usually leads to a hesitant growth flush and weaker branching within the crown.

Fan-shaped Growth

This trained growth form is particularly well-suited for our moderately cool climate. To ensure an even distribution of future main branches of the fan-shaped crown, it is beneficial to build a suitable frame or wall espalier 6-1/2 to 8 feet high (2-2.5m) before planting. The wires or slats used for fastening the shoots should be spaced 9-7/8" to 11-7/8" (25-30cm) maximum. To limit root formation (slowing growth), planting can be carried out in a pot (tub) or in a short concrete pipe (Ø 23-5/8" to 27-1/2 [60-70cm]). If

Prune fig plants before the growth flush.

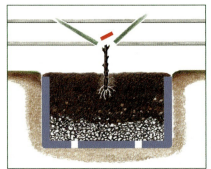

Two opposing branches form the main branch pair (top left). Heading cut in the spring of the second year (top right). Shoots that grow out over the crown must be shortened (bottom).

these are not available, a similar effect can be achieved by digging a hole 23-5/8" x 27-1/2" x 23-5/8" (60x70x60cm), which is then lined with stone or concrete slabs and filled with about 7-7/8" (20cm) of sandy gravel.

After planting, the stem elongation is cut back to around 15-3/4" to 19-3/4" (40-50cm). From the new summer shoots, two appropriate opposing limbs are attached to the framework as the first main branch pair. The rest of the shoots have to be removed.

In the spring of the second year, these two main shoots are again shortened to about half of their lengths. The new shoots now forming in the second vegetation period are used for the further buildup of the fan. Shoots that are growing toward the wall (from the crown), should either be removed immediately or be shortened to at least two to three leaves.

In the next year, and following years, this procedure should be repeated until the fan-shaped crown has reached the desired dimensions (after four to six years).

Two appropriate opposing branches are fastened to the framework as the first main branch pair.

> After the complete formation of the main network of branches, there is little pruning to be done. It is important to cut out all frost-damaged shoots and branches that are too thick or crossing one another.

Fall figs pictured above and flowering figs below.

With older trees, certain rejuvenation tasks have to be considered time and again. This should ensure that there is sufficient formation of younger shoots and at the same time the crown is kept light and less congested. The fig tree tolerates severe pruning quite well and new growth also forms again rather well from the old growth.

In late summer in our part of the world, small fruits develop on or near the ends of young shoots. After trees shed their leaves, these young figs (so-called flowering figs) stop growing. If these small fruits survive after mild winters or in protected locations, they will be fully formed the following spring and can be harvested in late summer. Surviving the winter depends on their thickness (stage of development), but mainly on the temperatures. After frosts of -39 to 41°F (- 4-5°C), they usually fall off.

From the second harvest, whose fruits develop on new shoots in spring, those that form the earliest ripen best and can then be harvested before the arrival of the first frost. These figs are called fall figs. By pinching young shoots between spring and mid-summer, lower buds are also stimulated to sprout and thus a balding of the crown is prevented.

IMPORTANT:

Young shoots are very prone to frost damage in the spring.

A beautifully grown candelabra pyramid with four base branches.

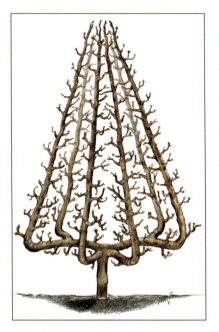

Candelabra pyramid without a supporting frame.

Other Espalier Shapes

In addition to the previously mentioned trained growth forms, which generally suffice for the hobby gardener, some other crown forms should be introduced that focus more on "adornment or display value" than on practical use. If the interested hobby fruit grower wants to create something special, then cultivating a winged pyramid (candelabra pyramid) or a kettle crown (bowl or vase shaped) will definitely get noticed by the neighbors. These forms require elaborate framework, but overall are not as difficult to grow as they might seem in the beginning. With the appropriate care, an excellent harvest can also be achieved. These growth forms have proven to be excellent, primarily with pome fruit trees.

Candelabra Pyramid (Winged Pyramid)

These crowns are usually grown with three, six or a maximum of eight branches.

> The size should not be projected too large since maintaining the balance of the crown becomes more and more difficult with the increasing number of lateral branches.

This form should be grown without a central leader. Because the center of the crown normally gets the best supply of nutrients, there is an inevitable slow down of growth and often uneven growth of lateral branches.

The framework for growing a candelabra pyramid consists of a strong, 8- to 10-foot-long tree post (central) with the necessary espalier wires dispatched from its top.

It is best to attach these shaping aids to short stakes that are hammered into the ground or to suitable bolted anchors. To tighten, the wooden stakes are hammered further into the ground or the bolted anchors are screwed down more.

> A strong-growing, one-year-old graft, with (or without) early shoots, is best for the planting.

Three or four branches are grown from the one-year-old graft in the first year.

If early shoots are already available, three of four of them, which have roughly the same size, are chosen for the formation of the base frame to ensure uniform development.

The stem elongation is then cut back just above the highest lateral shoot.

As the first shaping aid, three or four smaller stakes can be hammered into the ground with spacing of about 7-7/8" to 11-7/8" (20-30cm) and tied to the central post to ensure that the shoots are trained as horizontally as possible.

These stakes can then be tied to the outer stakes (anchors) and then serve to further shape the base frame. The diameter of the base circle is usually 3 to 4 feet (1-1.2m).

Another possible shaping aid is to attach two intersecting crossbeams about 15-3/4" to 19-3/4" (40-50cm) above the ground (illustration below, middle). The length of the crossbeams should be roughly 3 feet (1m). In much the same way, another crossbeam 23-7/8" to 27-1/2" (60-70cm) can be added at a height of at least 5 feet (1.5m) — this will improve stability and later growth. The crossbeams can be affixed with metal hoops for better stability.

In most cases, wires leading down from the top of the central post are sufficient for training the shoots upward, but it is important that they are always sufficiently tightened. Suitable new shoots are shaped slightly diagonally upward and outward in the first year.

> Three to four shoots are chosen for the base frame.

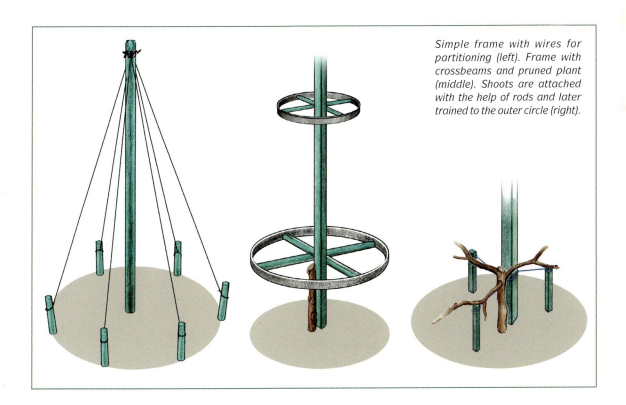

Simple frame with wires for partitioning (left). Frame with crossbeams and pruned plant (middle). Shoots are attached with the help of rods and later trained to the outer circle (right).

With the appropriate growth rate, the new shoots can already reach the periphery of the circle in the first year. Nevertheless, they are cut back again at the beginning of the second year to 9-7/8" to 11-7/8" (25-30cm) and only two sprouts are left for the further buildup of the crown.

These six (or eight) new shoots are eventually trained in the direction of the outer ring again. Thin rods or slats can be used to aid in the shaping.

IMPORTANT:

Crown shoots should develop at the same rate if possible. If this isn't the case, corrective pruning must be carried out (removing ends of ambitious shoots, for example). Weaker shoots, in contrast, can be trained somewhat more upright for now.

When the outer ring is reached, attach the crown branches and train upwards.

When the outer ring has been reached, the crown branches are then attached to the prepared wires and trained upward. If the shoots have balanced growth, they don't need to be pruned later. Otherwise, corrections must be made again in support of the weaker growing branches. Lateral shoot ends have to be removed (in July at the latest) after the fourth or fifth leaf to ensure further growth of the main shoot. Training the central leader does not apply to this crown form.

Kettle or Bowl Crown

Support frame for a bowl crown

Another, very similar trained crown form is the bowl or kettle crown. This form can be grown with six, twelve, or even twenty-four branches (and four, eight, or sixteen).

The construction of a practical frame is a requirement for this form too.

Depending on the planned size of the crown, three or six stronger stilts are hammered vertically into the ground; two to three metal rings are then attached around these stilts. The lowest ring should be about 15-3/4" to 19-3/4" (40-50cm) above the ground. The other metal hoops are spaced at around 31-1/2" (80cm). In doing so, a total height of about 6-1/2 to 8 feet (2-2.5m) will result. Thinner wooden slats, which will be used to train the crown branches later, are then attached vertically onto the metal rings at an appropriate distance between the stilts.

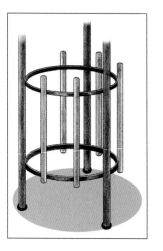

With this form too, a one-year-old graft (strong to medium-strength rootstock) is planted in the center of the ring and then cut back to about 11-7/8" to 15-3/4" (30-40cm).

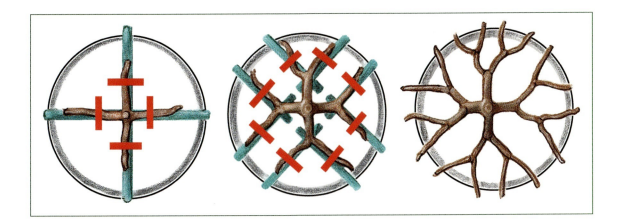

The highest three (or four) new developing shoots are trained slightly diagonally upward aided by flimsier rods in the direction of the lowest metal ring. In the following spring, the shoots are cut back to about 7-7/8" to 11-7/8" (20-30cm) of the new growth, each according to size. From the new shoots, only the two outer shoots should be left and then trained with the help of suitable rods in the direction of the metal ring and wooden stilts.

Kettle crown with 4, 8, or 16 branches in the base frame

> From the beginning on, care should be taken to ensure that all branches develop uniformly.

Even growth of a bowl-shaped crown

This can be achieved by positioning stronger branches horizontally at the right time, by shorter or longer pruning cuts or by the appropriate pinching of the shoots.

In the third year, all main shoots are cut back again to at least half of their length and again only the two outer shoots are left. After reaching the outer metal ring, the shoots are now attached vertically on the stilts and rods and trained upwards. The larger the number of crown shoots, the bigger the bowl form will inevitably become (a diameter up to 6-1/2' [2m]) and the more difficult it will become to ensure uniform development of all crown shoots.

> For the hobby gardener just starting our, the chances of success are higher with a smaller number of branches (six or eight).

Looseness (a somewhat larger spacing of branches) is also warranted and guarantees large-fruiting, high-yielding trees.

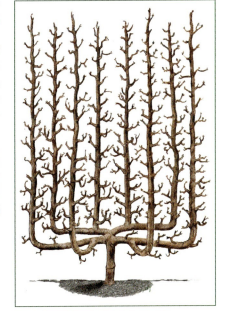

Spiral Cordon

Another form that remains open like the bowl-shaped crown is the so-called spiral cordon.

A frame consisting of four wooden stilts vertically positioned in the ground is used.

To improve the stability, two to three metal rings with a diameter of up to 3 feet (1m) can be fastened to the stilts at varying distances. The height of the stilt cylinders should not exceed 6-1/2 feet (2m) in order to assure later maintenance and harvesting tasks.

> A strong, one-year-old graft should be used for planting in the center of the cylinder. After planting in the spring, it is cut back to a height of about 9-7/8 to 11-7/8" (25-30cm).

Three or four suitable shoots that are left over after the growth flush of spring are trained slightly diagonally upward and outward to the lowest metal ring with the help of suitable shaping aids, which is similar to bowl-shaped crowns.

When the shoots have reached the lowest ring, they are attached to the rods and then shaped diagonally upward at an angle of about 45°.

For better distribution of shoots, stronger wires can also be utilized.

As soon as the height of the frame (about 6-1/2' [2m]) is reached, the shoot ends are removed and later diverted to weaker shoots.

> In order to be able to keep the form loose, the developing lateral shoots must have their ends removed during the summer to two to four leaves.

Should the opportunity arise, the framework can of course also be extended upward.

Frame for training a spiral cordon (top); a large spiral cordon with four main branches (bottom).

Variety Descriptions

Apples

Discovery

Origin: England; developed around 1950 from an open pollination of the Worcester Pearmain

Ripe for picking: From mid-August

Fruit: Small- to medium-sized; flat/roundish shaped

Skin: Intensely bright red color; waxy

Flesh: Whitish; aromatic; predominantly sweet; slightly tart

Blossoming: Mid-early

Harvest: Moderate; because of its clustered fruit set, it must be fertilized

Tree: Medium to weak; compact growth; forms a lot of short shoots, so thinning out is required; needs nutrient-rich, porous soils

Vulnerabilities: Somewhat susceptible to mildew; cracks can form in the area of the stem depression

Assessment: Due to its compact growth, it is optimally suited for espalier growth; attractive and flavorful apple variety

James Grieve

Origin: Scotland, since 1890

Ripe for picking: Mid-August, should be picked thoroughly

Fruit: Medium- to large-sized; roundish, somewhat asymmetrical with wide, soft ribs; very pressure sensitive

Peel: Smooth; waxy; greasy later on; streaked on sunny side or opaque red

Flesh: Fine, moderately firm texture; juicy, sweet, and tart with a typical aroma

Blossoming: Early and long-lasting; flowers appear on one-year-old long shoots

Harvest: Early onset and very high yield each year

Tree: Medium-strength growth, weak later on; compact growth

Vulnerabilities: In cool spring weather, frost rings appear on the fruits; susceptible to aphids

Assessment: Rich fruit-producing variety, which also prospers at higher altitudes in nutrient-rich soils; since the coloration of the standard variety is often unsatisfactory, one should resort to more intense red-colored hybrids

Geheimrat Dr. Oldenburg

Origin: Germany, 1897; result of a cross between Minister Hammerstein and Baumann's Reinette

Ripe for picking: Around the end of August

Fruit: Small and roundish to tall due to the high fruit set; slightly ribbed

Skin: Yellowish-green, smooth, greasy later on, with light red to sometimes dark red opaque

Flesh: Whitish-yellow; moderately firm, juicy, and slightly tart

Blossoming: Average; quite frost-hardy

Harvest: Early; regular and very high yield; fruits hang densely on tree

Tree: Due to the early onset of harvest, only medium-strength growth; requires nutrient-rich soils with adequate supply of water

Vulnerabilities: Wood is sensitive to low winter temperatures; somewhat susceptible to scabbing and mildew

Assessment: Only produces good fruit quality in protected, warm locations, as it is somewhat susceptible to wind; young fruiting spurs form through yearly pruning measures; like all early varieties, it has a short storage life

Goldparmäne

Origin: France, around 1590; also known as a Winter Goldparmäne

Ripe for picking: Beginning of September

Fruit: Small- to medium-sized, roundish

Skin: Greenish-yellow base color, orange-red on sunny side; coloring can be streaked to opaque

Flesh: Yellowish color; fine, firm texture; slightly sweet and very aromatic

Blossoming: Moderately late and usually long-lasting

Harvest: Medium to high yield; tends to be small fruit and must be thinned out

Tree: Medium-strength, but weak later, with short branch growth; well-suited for higher altitudes with the proper soil conditions; yearly pruning is necessary

Vulnerabilities: Somewhat susceptible to scarring and mildew

Assessment: Great for immediate fresh consumption; optimal pollinator for many apple varieties; the high vitamin C content makes this variety even more interesting

Gala

Origin: New Zealand; crossbreed of Kidd's and Golden Delicious

Ripe for picking: Beginning of September

Fruit: Medium-sized; somewhat tall build with wide, soft ribs around the fruit

Skin: Greenish-yellow base color; usually intensely streaked or opaque red; waxy

Flesh: Firm; predominantly sweet and slightly tart

Blossoming: Moderately late

Harvest: Very early; yield is regular and very high, so it must be thinned out

Tree: Medium-strength growth and branches well; forms a thick crown

Vulnerabilities: Cankers; tears open in the stem depression when watered excessively just before harvest.

Assessment: Attractive variety, of which there are several more intense red-colored hybrids; it stands out due to its very good storage life

Pinova

Origin: Germany, since 1986; created from cross between Clivia and Golden Delicious

Ripe for picking: End of September

Fruit: Medium-sized and roundish; tapers off near the calyx

Skin: Firm; greenish-yellow base cover, sunny side is orange-red

Flesh: Fine-grained, firm, cream-colored, sweet-sour

Blossoming: Moderately late

Harvest: Begins early; yield is high every year

Tree: Medium-strength growth; decreased, squarrose growth in full harvest; yearly pruning is necessary

Vulnerabilities: Somewhat susceptible to mildew; tends to re-bloom (risk of infection)

Assessment: Good, stable winter apple that requires sufficient humidity in storage, otherwise they begin to wilt; suitable for espaliers due to its weak growth, but shoots should be shaped in a non-lignified state; coloration occurs late; an intensely colored hybrid is being tested

Reinette de Champagne

Origin: France, around 1800; created from a chance seedling
Ripe for picking: Mid-October
Fruit: Small- to medium-sized; flat to flat-roundish shaped
Skin: Waxy, greasy later on; yellowish-white base color, sunny side orange-red
Flesh: Whitish-yellow color; juicy, refreshing, and slightly tart
Blossoming: Late; less susceptible to frost
Harvest: Begins early and is then regular; average yield
Tree: Medium-strength, weaker growth later on with short fruiting spurs; regular rejuvenating pruning is necessary
Vulnerabilities: Susceptible to cankers on wet, cold earth; scabbing in humid areas
Assessment: Good storage life; not ripe enough to eat before January due to the prevailing sourness (acidity); suitable acid donor for juice-making; ideal for espalier growing

Ananas Reinette

Origin: Most likely from the Netherlands
Ripe for picking: First half of October
Fruit: Small- to medium-sized and tall build
Skin: Yellowish, lemon-yellow later on; with numerous lenticel spots; sometimes an orange-red tint on the sunny side
Flesh: Firm and juicy with a slightly sour aroma
Blossoming: Moderately early; somewhat sensitive to weather conditions
Harvest: Begins early; yield is average; overhanging of this variety tends to cause small fruit (thinning out)
Tree: Weak-growing, thus regular pruning is necessary; needs protective, warm locations
Vulnerabilities: Susceptible to codling moth and mildew
Assessment: Popular, old variety that is also suitable for processing; fruits hang firmly to the fruiting spurs

London Pepping

Origin: England; well-known for over 400 years
Ripe for picking: First half of October
Fruit: Medium- to large-sized; flat-roundish with prominent ribbing around the calyx
Skin: Somewhat greasy; sunny side colored orange-red
Flesh: Whitish-yellow color; juicy, refreshingly sweet-sour, and aromatic
Blossoming: Moderately late; somewhat susceptible to bloom frost
Harvest: Begins early and produces high yields on a yearly basis
Tree: Medium-strength growth, weak later on; produces quality fruit in light, nutrient-rich soils.
Vulnerabilities: Somewhat susceptible to scabbing
Assessment: Good storage life and a very tasty variety; however, it requires adequate care

Pilot

Origin: Germany, since 1986; created from a cross between Clivia and Undine
Ripe for picking: End of September
Fruit: Medium-sized; flat-roundish with light ribbing around the calyx
Skin: Greenish-yellow, but in large part an intense bright red color
Flesh: Very firm and crispy; juicy, and refreshingly tart
Blossoming: Moderately late; frost-prone
Harvest: Regular and high yield
Tree: Medium-strength growth in the beginning, weak later on; branches grow horizontally and loosely.
Vulnerabilities: Somewhat susceptible to scabbing and mildew
Assessment: This variety doesn't achieve its full flavor until after several weeks in storage, but it has a very good storage life; table apple that is also suitable for processing

Topaz

Origin: Czech Republic, since 1994; cross between Rubin and Vandal

Ripe for picking: Last week in September

Fruit: Medium- to large-sized; flat-roundish and ribbed shaped

Skin: Firm; greenish-yellow at first, lemon-yellow when ripe with streaked to opaque redness around the entire fruit

Flesh: Firm; predominantly tart at harvest time; after a few weeks of storage, harmoniously sweet-sour and very refreshing

Blossoming: Early to moderately early

Harvest: Moderately high to high yield, but tends to alternate

Tree: Medium-strength growth; upright in its youth, broadening later

Vulnerabilities: Somewhat susceptible to mildew and aphids; sensitive to fire blight; large fruits are often spotted

Assessment: Excellent winter apple with very good storage qualities; mostly resistant to scabbing; requires nutrient-rich soils with good water supply; the most important variety in organic orchards

Pears

Precoce de Trevoux

Origin: France, found around 1860

Ripe for picking: End of July

Fruit: Medium-sized; piriform- to bell-shaped

Skin: Greenish-yellow base color; orange to reddish stripes on sunny side

Flesh: Juicy/half melting, slightly aromatic, sweet-sour

Blossoming: Average; resistant to unfavorable flowering conditions

Harvest: Begins early; moderate yield; fruits often small in size

Tree: Medium-strength growth in the beginning, weaker growth with hanging branches later on; good flower bud formation

Vulnerabilities: Somewhat susceptible to scabbing in humid areas

Assessment: Early pear of good quality, recommended due to its low susceptibility to disease; there is also a hybrid ("Super Trevoux" – a larger fruit with equally good characteristics)

Jules Gujot

Origin: France, since 1875

Ripe for picking: Mid-August

Fruit: Large-sized and long piriform-shaped

Skin: Moderately firm and smooth; yellowish-green base color, sometimes slightly red on sunny side

Flesh: Juicy, liquescent, slightly sweet-sour, and just a bit aromatic

Blossoming: Moderately early; less frost-prone

Harvest: Begins early; yield is average

Tree: Medium-strength growth, weak later on; yearly pruning is necessary since the tree degenerates otherwise and fruiting spur formation becomes unsatisfactory

Vulnerabilities: Somewhat susceptible to codling moth infestations; scabbing is rare; sensitive to copper treatments

Assessment: Attractive summer pear; an alternative to the Williams pear, but ripens somewhat early and is not as productive as the Williams pear

Williams Pear (Bartlett)

Origin: England, known since 1770

Ripe for picking: End of August

Fruit: Medium- to large-sized; piriform- to bell-shaped with warped surface

Skin: Smooth, undisturbed while eating; base color is yellowish-green, yellow later on, occasionally light orange

Flesh: Very juicy, liquescent, and refreshingly sweet-sour with a slight nutmeg flavor

Blossoming: Moderately early, less sensitive to weather conditions

Harvest: Begins early and is abundant every year

Tree: Medium-strength growth, weak later on; forms plenty of fruiting spurs

Vulnerabilities: Susceptible to scabbing; sensitive to copper sprays; more susceptible to fire blight

Assessment: World-renowned variety that fulfills all requirements taste-wise; the abundant fruit set demands regular pruning and should also be thinned out so that the quality is preserved; in addition to the Williams pear, there is a red Williams, which was created from a bud mutation

Gute Luise

Origin: France, since 1780
Ripe for picking: Beginning of September
Fruit: Medium- to occasionally large-sized; piriform-shaped
Skin: Greenish-yellow when ripe; sunny side reddish-brown, orange-red later on; typical for this variety is its lower positioned spots
Flesh: Very juicy, liquescent, and refreshingly sweet-sour with a fine aroma
Blossoming: Average
Harvest: Begins early and is moderately high; with overhanging branches, this variety tends to produce smaller fruit (thin out)
Tree: Strong growth in the beginning, slows at the onset of the harvest; yearly pruning is needed in later years
Vulnerabilities: Vulnerable to bloom frost; humid locations should be avoided due to susceptibility to scabbing; sensitive to copper and sulfur treatments
Assessment: Excellent fall pear with good storage qualities; also good for juice making when still firm

Conference

Origin: England, since 1895
Ripe for picking: Mid-September
Fruit: Medium-sized and bottle-shaped
Skin: Firm; greenish-yellow base color; often intensely russeted around the calyx area
Flesh: Yellowish-white color; juicy, liquescent, aromatic, and predominantly sweet
Blossoming: Moderately early
Harvest: Begins early and is moderately high later on; tends to overhang and must then be thinned out
Tree: Medium-strength growth, weak in the beginning; regular pruning of fruiting spurs; forms mainly short fruiting spurs
Vulnerabilities: Calcium content in soils leads to chlorosis, especially when combined with quince rootstocks
Assessment: This variety produces optimal quality only under good soil conditions; widespread in Western Europe; ripens very well in storage

Uta

Origin: Germany; created from a cross between Madame Verte and Bosc's Flaschenbirne; increased cultivation over the last ten years

Ripe for picking: Second half of September

Fruit: Medium- to large-sized and cone- to spinning top-shaped

Skin: Bronzed dark brown; base color rarely emerges; no reddening

Flesh: Juicy and liquescent with a refreshing aroma; pleasantly sweet-sour

Blossoming: Moderately early

Harvest: Begins early and is abundant every year

Tree: Medium-strength growth; forms sufficient side wood; incompatible with quince

Vulnerabilities: Sensitive to low winter temperatures

Assessment: A very good tasting pear, which unfortunately is not very attractive; increasingly grown organically since they are very resistant to scabbing

Alexander Lukas

Origin: Found in the forest near Blois, France, around 1870; in circulation ever since

Ripe for picking: End of September

Fruit: Medium- to very large-sized; pirifom- to cone-shaped; often roundish with sunk-in stem

Skin: Firm and smooth; greenish-yellow base color, orange-red on sunny side

Flesh: Juicy and liquescent with aromatic sweet-sour

Blossoming: Moderately early; less susceptible to weather conditions

Harvest: Yield is moderately high to high; tends to alternate

Tree: Medium-strength growth, later weak and hanging; shows good branching; yearly pruning is recommended

Vulnerabilities: Sensitive to bloom frosts; low susceptibility to scabbing

Assessment: This variety doesn't place any high demands on location; fruits are somewhat susceptible to wind; they have a good storage life, but it is a triploid variety and is, therefore, not a suitable pollination partner for other varieties

Plums

Herman

Origin: Sweden, 1952; created from a cross between The Czar and Ruth Gerstetter

Ripe for picking: From the second week in July, in series

Fruit: Medium-sized; roundish (prune-like)

Skin: Dark violet to dark blue when completely ripe

Flesh: Soft to moderately firm; very juicy, slightly spicy; pit easily removed

Blossoming: Average; self-fruitful

Harvest: Begins early; yield is high in the following years for an early variety

Tree: Medium-strength growth, forms a wide crown

Vulnerabilities: Susceptible to plum rust

Assessment: Interesting due to its early ripening; has a good tolerance to plum pox virus; repeated picking is required in order to harvest completely ripe fruits

Mirabelle von Nancy

Origin: Mainly grown in eastern France; known since the 18th century

Ripe for picking: Second half of August

Fruit: Small and roundish

Skin: Soft, yellow-gold; red spots on sunny side

Flesh: Firm, yellow, aromatic, sweet, mealy when over-ripe

Blossoming: Moderately late, self-fruitful; flowers are very frost-hardy

Harvest: Begins early; yield is always high

Tree: Medium-strength growth; forms a wide crown and lateral branches with short, thick fruiting spurs

Vulnerabilities: Only produces good quality in warm growing areas

Assessment: Fruits are very tasty and are suitable for every kind of processing; tolerant to plum pox virus

Jojo

Origin: Germany; created from a cross between Ortenauer and Stanley

Ripe for picking: Last week of August

Fruit: Large, dark blue; already intense coloring before full ripeness

Skin: Moderately firm, intensely frosted

Flesh: Firm and juicy; refreshingly tart plum aroma; pit easily removed

Blossoming: Average; self-fruitful

Harvest: Begins early; yield is average to high

Tree: Medium-strength growth, forms flat exit angles and branches well

Vulnerabilities: Average susceptibility to plum rust and plum fruit moths

Assessment: Large, very tasty variety that is plum pox resistant; great for cake topping

Valjevka

Origin: Former Yugoslavia; an approved variety since 1984

Ripe for picking: Beginning of September

Fruit: Medium-sized with a longish, plum-like shape

Skin: Dark blue, intensely colored

Flesh: Firm and very juicy; golden yellow color when fully ripe; the pits are easy to remove

Blossoming: Late; self-fruitful

Harvest: Begins early; yield is regular

Tree: Strong growth, medium-strength later on; wide crown; lateral branches are well-formed and adorned with short fruiting spurs

Vulnerabilities: Blossoming is susceptible to cool and wet weather; sensitive to plum pox virus

Assessment: Recommended as a replacement for the house plum since it is not as susceptible to plum pox; thinning out or heading cuts are necessary; suitable for eating fresh or as cake topping

Top 2000

Origin: Germany; created from an open pollination of the Stanley variety

Ripe for picking: Early- to mid-September, depending on area of cultivation

Fruit: Longish, typical plum shape

Skin: Firm; intense blue coloration

Flesh: Yellow; spicy and refreshingly sweet-sour; the pit is easily removed

Blossoming: Average; very resistant to light bloom frosts; self-fruitful

Harvest: Begins early; yield is always very high; thinning out is required almost every year

Tree: Medium-strength growth, weak later on; forms a wide crown

Vulnerabilities: Fruits tend to burst in heavy rain, increasing the risk of fruit monilinia (brown rot); susceptible to plum fruit moths

Assessment: Plum pox resistant variety of good quality; suitable for processing as well as eating fresh

Elena

Origin: Germany, Hohenheim University, created in 1980; cross between Fellenberg and Stanley

Ripe for picking: From the second week of September

Fruit: Oval; unequal halves

Skin: Medium-sized; dark blue, intensely frosted

Flesh: Yellow-green; very juicy and harmoniously sweet-sour with plum aroma; the pit is not always easy to remove

Blossoming: Moderately early; self-fruitful

Harvest: Begins early; regular to high yields every year

Growth: Strong in the beginning, medium-strength at the onset of harvest; good branching

Vulnerabilities: Somewhat susceptible to fruit monilinia

Assessment: Very good taste; very well-suited for processing as well as eating fresh; plum pox tolerant

Anna Späth

Origin: Hungary, introduced in 1875
Ripe for picking: Mid-September
Fruit: Medium-sized, almost roundish (also known as half-plum)
Skin: Violet to dark blue; very firm
Flesh: Yellow color; juicy and firm; sweet-sour taste; the pit is often difficult to remove
Blossoming: Average; self-fruitful; less susceptible to bloom frosts
Harvest: This variety needs a few years until it fruits satisfactorily, at which time it can be harvested in one picking
Tree: Medium-strength growth; in the following years, the shoots are adorned with thick positioned fruiting spurs; the wood shows good winter frost hardiness
Vulnerabilities: Fruits can burst in heavy rain; sawflies and moths can be a problem; late in season, ripening is often inadequate
Assessment: Interesting as a late-ripening variety; tolerant to plum pox virus; it can be processed as stewed fruit or marmalade, but is better suited for eating fresh

Apricots

Orange Red

Origin: New Jersey, USA
Ripe for picking: Beginning of July
Fruit: Medium-sized and roundish shaped
Skin: Moderately firm; base color orange; bright red on sunny side
Flesh: Firm and moderately juicy; slight apricot aroma
Blossoming: Average; self-sterile, requiring a pollination partner
Harvest: Begins early; average yields
Tree: Strong growth in the beginning, but soon decreases
Vulnerabilities: Susceptible to flower and fruit monilinia in moist years
Assessment: Very interesting early variety, but only produces the desired quality in apricot-suitable growing areas; regular shaping required

Rouges de Fournes

Origin: France; created from a chance seedling
Ripe for picking: From mid-July, in series
Fruit: Small, roundish, and somewhat angular shaped
Skin: Moderately firm; base color orange; sunny side speckled orange
Flesh: Moderately firm to firm; yellow-orange; moderately juicy with only a slight apricot aroma
Blossoming: Early; self-fruitful
Harvest: Begins early; yield is high every year
Tree: Strong growth in the beginning, medium-strength later on; lateral branches with abundant flower bud formation
Vulnerabilities: Somewhat susceptible to scabbing and flower monilinia; susceptible to plum pox
Assessment: The weaker growth that begins after the onset of the harvest makes growing as an espalier easier; however, it must be thinned out; due to the fruit size, it is ideal for apricot dumplings; good transportability

Goldrich

Origin: USA; also known by the name Jumbo Cot
Ripe for picking: Mid-July
Fruit: Large- to very large-sized; roundish shape
Skin: Firm; intense orange base color, rarely reddened
Flesh: Firm; apricot aroma when ripe; subtle sour taste
Blossoming: Early; since it is only partly self-fruitful, it needs a pollination partner
Harvest: Begins early; yield is always high
Tree: Strong growth, but exhibits good branching; yearly pruning is necessary later on to regulate fruiting spurs
Vulnerabilities: Susceptible to plum pox and flower monilinia
Assessment: A very tasty fruit; especially suitable for eating fresh

Apricot de Nancy

Origin: France; found at the beginning of the 18th century; today there are already several hybrids of this variety

Ripe for picking: From the third week in July

Fruit: Medium- to large-sized; egg-shaped

Skin: Firm; fine fuzz; base color is greenish-yellow; sunny side is slightly reddened

Flesh: Moderately firm; soft when fully ripe; predominantly sweet; aromatic

Blossoming: Moderate; self-fruitful

Harvest: Begins after a few years and is then average

Tree: Strong growth, but develops flat lateral branches with short fruiting spurs

Vulnerabilities: Somewhat susceptible to flower monilinia; fruits like to burst when it rains before harvest

Assessment: Very tasty; ripens well; suitable as table fruit as well as for processing; sometimes mealy at the beginning of over-ripeness

Hungary's Best

Origin: Hungary, from chance seedling found around 1870

Ripe for picking: From mid-July, in series

Skin: Firm; greenish-yellow to yellow base color; sunny side varies from orange-red to carmine red

Flesh: Moderately firm; juicy with an excellent apricot aroma

Blossoming: Moderately late; self-fruitful

Harvest: Begins late; alternates after a high yield year

Tree: Strong growth at the beginning, somewhat weaker after the harvest begins

Vulnerabilities: Susceptible to plum pox as well as flower and fruit monilinia

Assessment: Excellent fruit quality; main variety in Austria known as "Kosterneuburger"; pressure-sensitive when fully ripe; good for eating fresh and every kind of processing; today there are several hybrids of this variety that differ from the parent variety in earlier or later harvests

Kuresia

Origin: Germany, created from an unknown variety
Ripe for picking: Last week of July
Fruit: Medium-sized and roundish shaped
Skin: Moderately firm; yellow to orange-yellow base color; sunny side slightly reddened
Flesh: Soft to moderately firm; yellow; slightly sweet-sour
Blossoming: Moderately early; can be self-fruitful
Harvest: Begins early, but yield is only average
Tree: Medium-strength growth; looser crown build-up
Vulnerabilities: Susceptible to scabbing and somewhat susceptible to flower monilinia
Assessment: Immune to the plum pox virus; doesn't demand a lot from the growing area; recommended for home use only due to the soft fruit

Bergeron

Origin: France, created from a chance seedling around 1920
Ripe for picking: End of July, beginning of August
Fruit: Medium- to large-sized and plump
Skin: Firm; orange base color; sunny side mottled to opaque light red
Flesh: Firm; orange color; not very juicy, but slightly sour and aromatic
Blossoming: Moderately late; self-fruitful
Harvest: Begins early and is then regular every year and high
Tree: Strong growth at the beginning, moderate growth rate later on; ample flower bud garnishing
Vulnerabilities: Susceptible to flower monilinia and sensitive to plum pox
Assessment: Variety produces large, tasty fruit that ripen late; well-suited for eating fresh or processing; for optimal fruit development, it requires apricot-suitable growing areas; there is already a more intense reddened hybrid of this variety

Cherries

Bigarreau Burlat

Origin: France, created from a seedling
Ripe for picking: Beginning of July
Fruit: Large sized; heart- to kidney-shaped
Skin: Bright red, glossy
Flesh: Semi-firm; red; pleasantly sweet-sour and slightly aromatic
Blossoming: Moderately early; self-sterile, requiring a pollination partner
Harvest: Begins early; yield is high for an early variety
Tree: Strong growth in the first few years, then becomes weaker; branches very well
Vulnerabilities: Flowers are somewhat sensitive to frost
Assessment: Excellent quality for an early variety; firmer flesh than all other early varieties

Celeste

Origin: Summerland, Canada, since 1980
Ripe for picking: Second week of June
Fruit: Large- to very large-sized
Skin: Dark red and glossy
Flesh: Moderately firm; juicy; very tasty
Blossoming: Moderately early; self-fruitful
Harvest: Begins early; average yield
Growth: Moderate growth rate; forms steep shoots, which should be shaped as long as they are not lignified
Vulnerabilities: Large fruits burst easily in rain just before the harvest
Assessment: Early variety that does not require a pollination partner; grub-free due to early ripeness

Samba

Origin: Summerland, Canada
Ripe for picking: Second week of June
Fruit: Large- to very large-sized, heart-shaped
Skin: Firm and intensely glossy
Flesh: Dark red-colored flesh; harmoniously sweet-sour and aromatic
Blossoming: Moderately early; said to be partly self-fruitful
Harvest: Begins early; yield is high every year
Tree: Medium-strength growth; forms strong lead shoots that only branch moderately
Vulnerabilities: Susceptible to black cherry aphids and somewhat prone to bursting
Assessment: Large fruiting variety with very good taste; wood and buds are winter frost hardy; abundant flowering every year thins itself out well

Large Princess Cherry

Origin: Germany, known for over 250 years
Ripe for picking: Mid-July
Fruit: Medium- to large-sized and heart-shaped
Skin: Firm; yellow to orange-yellow base color; sunny side carmine red
Flesh: Firm; "crispy" and refreshingly sweet-sour; good aroma, but juice is not colored
Blossoming: Average; self-sterile, requiring a pollination partner
Harvest: Begins early; yield is high
Tree: Strong growth at first, medium-strength later on; also develops hanging branches later on
Assessment: This variety is a rarity due to its fruit color; for eating fresh, but also for processing; especially suitable for stewed fruit

Van

Origin: Summerland, Canada, arrived in Europe fifty years ago
Ripe for picking: Mid-June
Fruit: Medium- to large-sized; kidney-shaped
Skin: Glossy with subtle dotting
Flesh: Firm; bright red; sweet-sour and aromatic; juice-colored
Blossoming: Moderately early, self-sterile, a suitable pollination partner is necessary
Harvest: Begins early; yield is regularly high
Growth: Strong growth at first, but decreases quickly; branches very well; lateral branches with thick positioned bouquet branches
Vulnerabilities: Thick positioned fruits are prone to bursting
Assessment: Excellent table fruit; the short stem makes picking more tedious than other varieties; the rich, almost yearly fruit set should be thinned out

Hedelfinger

Origin: Seedling from Hedelfingen (near Stuttgart)
Ripe for picking: End of July
Fruit: Medium-sized and heart-shaped
Skin: Bright cherry red- to dark red-colored
Flesh: Firm; sweet, slightly sour, and aromatic; juice-colored
Blossoming: Moderately late; requires pollination partner
Harvest: Begins later, but yield is high and regular
Growth: Upright in the first few years, hanging later on; lateral branches have abundant flower buds
Vulnerabilities: Bursts quite easily
Assessment: No high location demands; good for eating fresh and processing; there are also later ripening versions of this variety

Hybrid Cherries

Queen Hortensie

Origin: Unknown
Ripe for picking: Mid-July
Fruit: Medium- to large-sized; oval-shaped
Skin: Thin; yellow base color; sunny side orange-red colored
Flesh: Soft; very juicy and aromatic; harmoniously sweet-sour
Blossoming: Average; self-sterile
Harvest: Begins late; yield is average
Tree: Medium-strength growth, weak later on with hanging branches
Vulnerabilities: Susceptible to flower monilinia; skin browns quickly
Assessment: Good variety for fruit lovers; it is suitable for fresh eating, but needs protected locations

Sour Cherries

Köröser II

Origin: Hungary, early ripening selection from the Köröser group
Ripe for picking: Mid-July
Fruit: Medium- to large-sized; flat and roundish-shaped
Skin: Semi-firm; very juicy and pleasantly sweet-sour; fine aroma; juice is strongly colored
Harvest: Begins early; yield is average
Growth: Strong, medium-strength later on; only moderate bareness of branches
Vulnerabilities: Somewhat susceptible to flower monilinia; ripe fruits burst easily in the rain
Assessment: Primarily suitable for eating fresh, but also for processing; only produces satisfactory harvests if blooming and pollination proceed optimally

Karneol

Origin: Germany, since 1990; created from a cross between Köröser and Schattenmorelle

Ripe for picking: Beginning of July

Fruit: Medium- to large-sized

Skin: Semi-firm; brown/red- to dark brown/red-colored; finely dotted

Flesh: Intense red coloring; pleasantly sweet-sour

Blossoming: Average; partly self-fruitful

Harvest: Begins early; yield is average

Tree: Strong growth at the beginning, weaker after a few years; develops a wide crown; lateral branches hanging; bareness is not as prevalent as with morello cherries

Vulnerabilities: Somewhat sensitive to bloom frosts

Assessment: Ideal fruit for processing, but also for eating fresh; ideal for subsistence farming; protected areas are recommended; its strong growth rate can be reduced by using weaker growing rootstocks

Peaches

Mayflower

Origin: USA, available worldwide since 1930

Ripe for picking: Beginning of July

Fruit: Medium-sized

Skin: Semi-firm; fuzzy, greenish-yellow base color; sunny side opaque red

Flesh: Whitish-green; reddened around the pit; aromatic; pit cannot be removed

Blossoming: Moderately early; self-fruitful

Harvest: Begins early, but yields are only average

Tree: Strong growth, decreases with age

Vulnerabilities: Low susceptibility to leaf curl

Assessment: Early peach with a good aroma; very frost hardy; location demands are low

Redhaven

Origin: Michigan, USA, since 1940
Ripe for picking: Beginning of August
Fruit: Medium- to large-sized
Skin: Semi-firm with fine fuzz; easy to peel; light yellow to yellow base color; carmine to dark reddening
Flesh: Bright yellow, firm and juicy; harmoniously sweet-sour with characteristic peach aroma
Blossoming: Average; self-fruitful
Harvest: Begins early; yield is high every year with the appropriate care
Tree: Medium-strength growth and very adaptable
Vulnerabilities: Susceptible to plum pox and leaf curl, but not as sensitive as other varieties
Assessment: The first peach with completely removable pit; excellent quality; the most important variety in peach-growing

Vineyard Peach

Origin: Usually grown from seedlings; today various selections are offered in nurseries
Ripe for picking: Depending on the type, from the beginning of August
Fruit: Small- to medium-sized; roundish shaped
Skin: Fuzzy, green base color; sunny side light red- to glowing red-colored
Flesh: Greenish to whitish-green; very juicy with a very good peach aroma
Blossoming: Average; self-fruitful
Harvest: Begins early; yield is always high, so thinning out is absolutely necessary
Tree: Medium-strength growth; pruning is necessary every year
Vulnerabilities: Susceptible to plum pox
Assessment: A very tasty fruit, but normally not very attractive; tends to produce small fruit; yearly pruning is necessary

Ellerstadt Red

Origin: Germany, around 1870; created from a chance seedling
Ripe for picking: From the beginning of September
Fruit: Medium- to large-sized; oval-shaped
Skin: Greenish-yellow to yellow base color; sunny side carmine red-colored; fuzzy; easy to peel
Flesh: Firm; greenish-white; juicy; sour with a slight aroma; pit easy to remove
Blossoming: Moderately late; self-fruitful
Harvest: Begins slowly, but yield is then average to high
Growth: Strong, medium-strength later on
Vulnerabilities: Low susceptibility to leaf curl and fruit monilinia
Assessment: Low demands on location and climate; well-suited for fruit stew processing

Gooseberries

Höning's Earliest

Origin: Germany, since 1900
Ripe for picking: End of July
Fruit: Medium-sized; roundish- to oval-shaped
Skin: Yellow; thin, fine bristles
Flesh: Soft with a predominantly sweet and slightly sour taste; pleasant aroma
Blossoming: Early; self-fruitful; additional pollination partners produce a better fruit set
Harvest: Average; yield fluctuates
Growth: Strong and upright; regular pruning necessary
Vulnerabilities: Moderately susceptible to mildew; sensitive to winter frost
Assessment: Very tasty variety; does not demand a lot from soils; suitable for eating fresh; pressure sensitive

Remarka

Origin: Germany, since 1970
Ripe for picking: First half of June
Fruit: Medium-sized; roundish-shaped
Skin: Dark red color; thin with little fuzz
Flesh: Very juicy; refreshingly sweet-sour; good gooseberry aroma
Blossoming: Early to moderate; self-fruitful
Harvest: Average
Growth: Medium-strength to weak; compact; regular pruning necessary
Vulnerabilities: Low susceptibility to mildew; fruits burst in rain, requiring several thorough pickings
Assessment: Very good taste for an early ripening variety

Invicta

Origin: East Malling, England
Ripe for picking: From mid-July
Fruit: Medium-sized; roundish to slightly tall-shaped
Skin: Light green; thin with little fuzz; fine bristles
Flesh: Greenish-yellow; sweet, slightly sour, harmonious taste and good aroma
Blossoming: Average; self-fruitful
Harvest: Yield is high and regular
Growth: Strong and upright
Vulnerabilities: Low susceptibility to mildew; sensitive to little space
Assessment: Very well suited for hedge growth; ideal for the home garden

Rexrot

Origin: Germany, since 1999; created from chance seedling

Ripe for picking: From mid-July

Fruit: Medium- to large-sized; roundish shape

Skin: Brownish-red base color; sunny side bright red color; semi-firm with very little fuzz

Flesh: Pleasantly sweet-sour with refreshing gooseberry aroma

Blossoming: Moderately early; self-fruitful

Harvest: Yield is high and regular

Growth: Medium-strength; upright at first and then spread wide later on

Vulnerabilities: Low susceptibility to mildew; fruits are really burst resistant

Assessment: A very attractive fruit; very robust; suitable for the home garden

Red Currants

Rovada

Origin: The Netherlands, since 1970

Ripe for picking: End of July

Fruit: Berries are consistently spherical and in long clusters

Skin: Glossy, bright red color

Flesh: Aromatic with a sour note

Blossoming: Late; self-fruitful

Harvest: High to very high yield

Growth: Medium-strength; bushy

Vulnerabilities: Low susceptibility to gall mites; rarely tends to drop

Assessment: Suitable for eating fresh and processing; ideal for hedge growth; rain-proof

Black Currants

Titania
Origin: Sweden, since 1985
Ripe for picking: Second half of June
Fruit: Medium- to large-sized; long clusters
Skin: Matte/glossy, black color
Flesh: Aromatic with sour taste
Blossoming: Average; self-fruitful
Harvest: High to very high yield
Growth: Strong; upright and broad
Vulnerabilities: Low susceptibility to blister rust; somewhat susceptible to mildew and mites; rarely tends to drop
Assessment: Rich-bearing variety for all forms of processing; yield and quality of fruits increase with good soil conditions

Blackberries

Black Satin
Origin: Illinois, USA
Ripe for picking: From the end of July
Fruit: Medium-sized; roundish- to oval-shaped
Skin: Glossy black; semi-firm
Flesh: Juicy, soft, and refreshing
Blossoming: Average; self-fruitful, but additional pollination partners produce a better fruit set
Harvest: Average to high yield
Growth: Strong; shoots without prickles
Vulnerabilities: Somewhat susceptible to botrytis
Assessment: Fruits have many uses; ripen until November; also suitable for the home garden

Nessy

Origin: Dundee, Scotland
Ripe for picking: From the end of July
Fruit: Medium-sized; oval-shaped, wider at the base of the fruit
Skin: Firm; glossy black color
Flesh: Sweet-sour taste with blackberry aroma
Blossoming: Early; self-fruitful
Harvest: Yield is moderately high and regular
Growth: Strong; develops prickle-free tendrils up to 10 feet long (3m)
Vulnerabilities: Low susceptibility to fruit rot; somewhat susceptible to downey mildew
Assessment: Produces large fruits and is a very tasty variety, which also has many uses; good for home gardens; winter frost hardy

Theodor Reimers

Origin: From the Himalaya region, introduced to Germany around 1900 by Theodor Reimers
Ripe for picking: From the beginning of August, in series
Fruit: Small- to medium-sized; somewhat non-uniform in size; roundish-shaped
Skin: Semi-firm, glossy black color
Flesh: Juicy and refreshingly sweet-sour with an intense blackberry aroma
Blossoming: Average; self-fruitful
Harvest: Yield is moderately high to high
Growth: Strong-growing; vigorous tendril growth; branches well, but has a lot of sharp prickles
Vulnerabilities: Somewhat susceptible to fruit rot; sensitive to winter frost
Assessment: Only fully ripened fruits have the prominent blackberry aroma; best suited for processing

Grapes

Queen of the Vineyard

Origin: Hungary; known for almost 100 years
Ripe for picking: End of August
Fruit: Large berries, roundish- to oval-shaped
Skin: Firm
Flesh: Greenish-yellow; sweet taste with a slight nutmeg aroma
Blossoming: Moderately early
Harvest: High yield
Growth: Strong; trimming in every form possible
Vulnerabilities: Somewhat susceptible to powdery and downey mildew
Assessment: Early ripening table grapes; few problems with the cultivation

Gutedel

Origin: Said to have originated in Turkey; found throughout the world today
Ripe for picking: First half of September
Fruit: Large berries, slightly cone-shaped
Skin: Thin; yellow- to gold yellow-colored
Flesh: Sweet, pleasant aroma
Blossoming: Moderately late
Harvest: Yield is high and regular
Growth: Strong
Vulnerabilities: Susceptible to peronospora and oidium; grapevine moth infestations can also occur
Assessment: Needs locations that protect from late frost; excellent table grape

Kiwis

Hayward

Origin: Named after Hayward Wright, it became a selection in 1950; it is grown worldwide today

Ripe for picking: End of October

Fruit: Large, cylindrical shape

Skin: Pelt-like brown fuzz; easy to peel

Flesh: Green-colored; juicy and refreshing

Blossoming: June; pure female, pollinator is needed

Harvest: Yield is high to very high

Growth: Strong

Vulnerabilities: Ripens only in protected locations

Assessment: Recommended due to its high yield and fruit size; good storage life; high vitamin C content

In recent years, varieties have arrived on the market with male and female flowers on one plant. Well-known varieties are Jenny or Solo. Although they are self-fruitful this way and require less space, a pollinating variety produces better harvests. The fruits of these varieties are smaller and ripen in October. They grow to about the size of nuts. The yields are average.

The Major Diseases of Fruit Trees

Animal pests, fungal pathogens, and physiological diseases increasingly appear on fruit trees when the soil and climate conditions are not suitable. Pruning and shaping work should be coordinated on schedule so that the vegetative and generative development of the fruit trees is well balanced and their health is preserved.

Apples

Aphids

Aphids are often found in fruit trees. They spend the winter in the cracks or bark of tree trunks.

Rosy apple aphids, rosy leaf-curling aphids, and green apple aphids, in particular, cause massive damage to apple trees. Due to their rapid reproduction, severe rippling of leaves often results. Fruits are also deformed by the feeding activities of the rosy apple aphid.

The rosy leaf-curling aphid, on the other hand, causes an intense reddening of leaves (see illustration top of page 136).

The green apple aphid causes severe leaf wrinkling in the summer, whereby the shoot ends can be crippled and even die off.

Useful insects — like the green lacewing, hoverfly, or ladybug, to mention just a few — can considerably reduce aphids.

Glue rings, which are placed around fruit tree trunks, can prevent the upward movement of ants that aid in the spread aphids. If the degree of infestation is too high, spraying is necessary. Today there are organic as well as synthetic compounds available.

Wooly Apple Aphid

Wooly apple aphids are mainly found in the area of pruning cuts, trunk injuries and on roots, and they are also found in warmer growing areas. They are easy to recognize due to their whitish, waxy coat. If they are squashed, a red juice is excreted, which is why their German name is "blutlaus," meaning blood aphid.

A direct adversary is aphelinus mali (a parasitoid wasp), but earwigs and lady bugs can also reduce aphids.

In locations susceptible to wooly apple aphids, apple rootstocks, such as **MM 106** or **MM 111**, should be used since they are resistant to these aphids.

Winter Moths

The caterpillars of winter moths are found on all fruit tree varieties. The feeding damage to leaves and small fruits can lead to complete defoliation of fruit trees. The caterpillars of the small winter moth, in particular, cause great damage. If they have completed their development, they leave the fruit trees and pupate in the ground.

In order to prevent the oviposition of wingless females, which takes place beginning in October, glue rings should be placed around the trunk.

The majority of these pests can be intercepted this way. However, the glue rings need to be repeatedly tested since females can climb up well into November if the weather is warm.

If, despite the glue rings, these pests appear on leaves in the spring, treatments with a bacillus thuringiensis-based agent should be carried out during daytime temperatures above 59°F (15°C), depending on the degree of infestation.

Apple Blossom Weevil

Apple blossom weevils are found on apple and pear trees even before flowers open. These beetles lay their eggs in the opening buds and within ten days the larvae hatch from the eggs and begin to devour blossom organs and flower petals. As a result, the blossoms can no longer open and they turn brown.

A weaker infestation by these pests can even have a desirable, thinning-out effect with abundant blossoming.

Apple Sawfly

The flight of the apple sawfly begins during warm weather at the time of the bloom. The females each lay an egg under the sepals after they have made a cut in the flower's receptacle. Depending on weather conditions, it can last one to two weeks until the larvae hatch from the eggs. The larvae then eat through to the core of the small fruits and damage the seed structures. Later on, these fruits fall off the tree.

Because the larvae of apple sawflies infest several fruits during their development, enormous damage can result. If the cores are not eaten, the fruits continue to develop. At harvest time, one can see the prominent, corked traces of feeding, which can run from the calyx over the entire fruit.

Because this wasp species is attracted to the white color of flowers during the blooming period, the use of white glue panels helps to trap them.

A chemical treatment takes place at the end of flowering.

The larvae infest several fruits!

Bark Beetle

Bark beetles enter through untreated wounds in fruit trees.

The various species of bark beetles cause damage to all fruit tree varieties. They enter fruit trees through injuries on trunks and branches and through untreated wounds. Therefore, they are referred to as secondary pests.

Treating injuries and wounds with a coating agent is a preventative measure against bark beetles.

Codling Moth

Probably the most problematic pests for apple trees are the codling moths that also damage pears. This moth appears with two generations per year. Oviposition can be expected already in June with night temperatures around 59°F (15°C). Caterpillars hatch out of the eggs that are individually deposited on fruits or leaves and eat into the center of the fruit.

After the maturation feeding, which can last four weeks and passes through five developmental stages, they leave the fruit to pupate in the cracks of bark or in another suitable location. By the end of July to the beginning of August, the second generation can be expected, which can further damage the fruit.

Placing strips of corrugated board around the fruit tree trunk in June, before the caterpillars pupate, gives them the opportunity to pupate there. Through continuous monitoring, a portion of the pests can be intercepted and infestation by the second generation can be reduced.

Determine the beginning of flight and the intensity with pheromone traps.

By hanging pheromone traps (lures that attract males who then remain stuck to a glue panel), the beginning of flight and the intensity are determined in order to engage with insecticides or compounds that will prevent further development of these pests.

Useful insects, such as earwigs that eat deposited eggs, titmice, and woodpeckers that search tree trunks for food, also reduce the infestation by the second generation.

Fruit Tree Spider Mites

Fruit tree spider mites, which are about 1/100" (0.5mm) in size, primarily damage the bottom of leaves through their feeding activities. The leaves then lighten considerably. In winter, their red-colored eggs are found near buds or on the underside of branch forks. The larvae hatch in mid-April, and the warmer and drier the weather is, the faster they reproduce. The larvae develop into males and females who ensure several populations over the course of the vegetation period.

Treatment with an expellant spray should be carried out in the vegetative dormant period.

Phytoseiulus (predator mites), which are a natural adversary of the spider mite, can be purchased and are an environmentally-friendly pest control method.

Apple Scab

Apple scab is one of the diseases that chiefly cause damage to apples, but can also damage pears trees. The ascomycota fungus spends the winter in the previous year's foliage. Infection can already occur when budding begins. At first, oily spots appear on the young leaves and then the fruits are also infested. The damaged tissues die and the fruits tear open if they continue to grow. Apple scab infections continue until the growth period has ended.

To combat apple scab, preventative measures should be the main focus. Infected leaves need to be removed in the fall. In addition to the appropriate choice of location, the proper variety should also be resolved.

Tolerant or resistant varieties are preferred so that extensive spraying measures can be avoided.

Mildew (see illustration top of page 140)

Shoot ends with a whitish coating indicate a mildew attack. Developing leaves and flowers can be affected. Mildew spores spend the winter on buds and trigger the first infections during the growth flush. During severe winter frosts, the buds, upon which the spores develop, can die.

Temperatures of 59°F to 77°F (15-25°C) are crucial to the severity of infection. Higher humidity also promotes spore development.

> Pest control measures, like with apple scab control, are very complex, so choosing a variety that is mildew tolerant, resistant, or at least less susceptible should be considered.

Fruit Rot

Fruit rot can appear during vegetation, but also while in storage. The spores of this fungus enter through wounds that are caused by insects or hail or through lenticels in fruits. Because they hibernate in fruit mummies, in windfall fruit or on shoots, plant-hygienic measures, such as removing rotten fruit and pruning infected shoots and branches, are important.

> Fruits for storage should not be harvested when they are damp. Even injuries that occur during the harvest, such as ripping out the stem or wounds by fingernails, should be avoided.

Fire Blight

Fire blight is a bacterial disease that affects pome fruits as well as ornamental trees. It is difficult to control and highly infectious. Fire blight is transmitted by pruning tools, work clothes, birds, insects, and even by the wind and rain.

Initial infections can already appear during the spring bloom on flowers and leaves, which turn brown and, later on, black. Eventually, a bacterial slime oozes out. Under the bark, the wood turns a reddish-brown color. Only when the vegetation period ends, does the spread come to a halt.

> When the first symptoms appear, affected areas need to be identified. Infected branches and shoots have to be cut back to the healthy wood and burned. Pruning tools can be cleaned with an alcohol solution or disinfected with the flame of a blow torch. Shoes and work clothes should also undergo a cleaning.

Pears

Pear Rust Mite

The pear rust mite is a microscopic animal that hibernates in bud scales and becomes active when the growth flush begins. They suck on leaves and also lay their eggs there. Initial damage occurs on the bottom of the leaf. Pock marks are a typical indication of an infestation. After gall begins to form, in which reproduction takes place, pest control is no longer possible.

> Sulfur-based sprays are carried out during the dormant period in winter or during the growth flush at the latest.

Pear Sucker

Leaves and flowers can already be damaged by the feeding activities of the pear sucker during the growth flush. Shoot growth of young pear trees, in particular, is slowed considerably by these pests. Up to three generations can develop over the course of the vegetation year. They secrete honeydew on fruits, leaves, and shoots, which become sticky. A sooty mold fungus then colonizes there causing the fruits to become black and unsightly as well.

> The only natural adversary is the anthocoridae (flower bug). If massive damage occurs, an insecticide that spares beneficial insects should be employed.

Pear Midge

In recent years, pear midges have appeared in increasing numbers on pear trees. The females of this species often lay up to thirty eggs in a single flower.

> When the larvae hatch after a few days, they develop inside the small fruits, which then turn black and fall to the ground. These pests spin themselves into a cocoon within the fruit and spend the winter in the ground.

The larvae develop inside the small fruits.

A chemical treatment should be carried out just before blossoming.

Pear Rust

The first spore clusters of pear rust are visible by mid-June in humid weather. The spore clusters develop during the summer and then shift to juniper trees in the fall, where they hibernate for the winter. This is why it is also referred to as a host-changing rust fungus.

> The best control strategy is to clear the juniper trees, which interrupts the chain of development.

For chemical pest control, a fungicide should be used beginning in mid-May and in humid weather.

Plums

Aphids

Aphids appear very early. The first colonies can already be found at the beginning of the growth flush. As a result, rippling of leaf edges occurs, which considerably inhibits growth. Other species can cause early defoliation due to their feeding activities. The honeydew secretion of the aphid also causes sticky leaves on which the sooty mold fungus can develop uninhibited.

> In addition to useful insects, such as shield bugs, lady-bugs, or lacewings, which eat aphids, expellant sprays can be used to combat the hibernating aphid species.

Aphids are rather problematic with this fruit variety because they are also transmitters of the plum pox virus.

Plum Sawfly

Plum sawflies are attracted by the intense white color of a plum tree's flowers. The females lay an egg in the flower's receptacle and after the larvae hatch they eat into the small fruits. Because they damage a number of fruits during their development, total loss can even occur. When they are mature, they fall to the ground and hibernate there in a cocoon.

Typical damages are black holes on the fruits.

White glue panels helps reduce the risk of infestation.

Chemical control measures have to be carried out before the end of the flowering period.

Plum Fruit Moth

Plum fruit moths cause massive damage in warm growing areas. Like the codling moth, two generations can be expected. Females lay their first eggs by the end of May. After hatching, the caterpillars feed on the fruit flesh. Damaged fruits turn blue and fall to the ground, where the insects then cycle through their last stage of development.

Next, they hide in a cocoon behind bark flakes or in cracks in order to fly back to the fruits weeks later and lay the eggs of the second generation. The beginning of flight and the flight intensity of these moths can be determined by using pheromone traps.

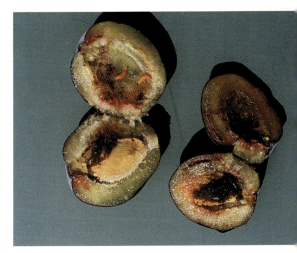

Insecticides or developmental inhibitors are successful control alternatives. Fallen fruit of the first generation should be collected as quickly as possible since the caterpillars can still be located inside them.

Plum Pox Virus

The plum pox virus presents a huge problem for plums and prunes. In addition, apricots, peaches, and nectarines can also be affected. This viral disease can only be controlled by uprooting infected trees. The only preventative measure that makes sense is spraying to control the aphids that spread the virus through their feeding activities.

Typical damages are light green, ring-shaped patches on the leaves. On fruits, pock-like depressions on the skin can occur. In severe infestations, the flesh of the fruit turns reddish and becomes rubbery. Premature fruit falling is also characteristic of an infestation.

Healthy fruit trees are only grown over virus-free materials. Today there are varieties that are virus resistant or have a high tolerance to these diseases.

Plum Pockets

Plum pockets can cause enormous loss of plum yields. Infections can occur as early as the blooming period in cool and moist weather conditions. Weeks later, the fruits turn white and then later become brown and have a pod-like shape. The surface is wrinkled, yellowish-gray, and later brown-colored.

Collecting the fallen fruits is the only sensible plant-hygienic measure at this point. Fungicide sprays only have the desired effect during the blooming period.

Plum Rust

Infection by plum rust occurs at the end of May or early June in humid weather. The first yellow-colored spore clusters are found on the bottom of leaves. This disease spreads quickly through continuous new infections. With an early attack, plum trees can lose their leaves as early as August. Not only is the ripening of later varieties endangered by this, but also flower development.

The main cause of infection is fallen leaves. Spores hibernate in them and ensure another infection the next year.

Infections can also be carried out by anemone growths, but removing these plants can't control this fungal disease.

Fungicide sprays are necessary in cool, moist weather beginning in mid-June.

Apricots

Bark Beetles
Infestation by various bark beetle species occurs through injuries and untreated wounds.

Proper tree maintenance can prevent these pests from entering fruit trees.

Aphids
Aphids seldom attack apricot trees, but through their feeding activities they are transmitters of diseases -- predominantly plum pox virus and apricot chlorotic leaf roll.

Aphids are transmitters of diseases.

Plum Pox Virus
Plum pox infection of apricots is similar to that of plums and prunes (described on page 144).

Chlorotic Leaf Roll
Chlorotic leaf roll of apricots has already spread worldwide. Typical symptoms of this phytoplasmose are cone-shaped, curled-up leaves, weaker growth, and inferior fruits. Defoliation also begins prematurely and, consequently, the trees die off.

A precise diagnosis of this disease is only possible through laboratory tests.

Once a tree is infected, it can only be uprooted.

Monilinia of Flowers and Shoot Ends

Apricots and sour cherries are increasingly being infected by monilinia. In humid weather, massive damage can occur on flower organs and on branches since the fungus also penetrates wood. A typical sign for an infection is the discharge of pitch at the junction of healthy to damaged shoot.

> Removing the affected portion of shoot and the fruit mummies in the fall is necessary because they will be the source of next year's infection.

Apoplexy

Apoplexy, also called heat stroke, has many causes. When choosing a location, late-frost areas, cold, heavy soils, and soils with high groundwater levels should be avoided. Inappropriate rootstocks lead to affinity problems. Annually appearing diseases and nourishment mistakes can also be a cause of heat stroke.

> Improper pruning also leads to apoplexy.

Sweet and Sour Cherries

Black Cherry Aphids

Damage to shoot ends on cherry trees is caused by black cherry aphids. In addition to their feeding activities on leaves, they also excrete honey dew, which makes the fruits sticky and, thus, inedible.

> If only a few shoot ends are infected, aphids can be controlled by cutting off the affected parts.

Severe infection should be treated with an insecticide.

Cherry Fruit Flies

Probably the most unpleasant pests of this fruit variety are the maggots of cherry fruit flies. Only the early varieties are ripe before the maggots hatch. In cherry varieties that ripen from the third cherry week, small, barely visible maggots can be found. A few days later, when they have completed their development, the fruits are no longer suitable for eating or processing.

By hanging adhesive traps on the south side of the cherry trees on or around May 20th, the beginning of flight, intensity of flight, and the point of oviposition can be determined. The eggs are laid under the skin when the color of the fruits changes from green to yellow.

> Because several adhesive traps per cherry tree are not sufficient for controlling these pests, a targeted insecticide spray should be carried out.

Cylindrosporium Leaf Spot

In humid weather conditions, the initial damage caused by cylindrosporium leaf spot can already appear in June. Roundish, brown- to violet-colored spots develop on the top side of leaves. The leaves then become yellow and fall off. In years with high rainfall amounts, new infections are possible up until August.

In the case of an early infection and premature defoliation, fruits will no longer ripen.
Damaged shoots lignify poorly and then freeze off in winter. The development of flower buds is also jeopardized.

If this fungal disease occurs annually, the vitality of sweet and sour cherry trees is affected.

> Removing infected leaves and cutting off damaged shoots are preventative measures against this fungal disease.

Targeted fungicide treatments beginning in the second half of May can also successfully control cylindrosporium leaf spot.

Shot Hole Disease

Humid cultivation conditions in spring enable the spread of shot hole disease. Soon after the growth flush, red spots appear on leaves, which then get bigger. Leaf tissue dies off and falls out. Hence, the name "shot hole." Sunken spots are found on fruits, which then wrinkle and dry up.

Shoots also emit a rubbery discharge.

> If this fungal disease occurs annually, branches or entire cherry trees can die.

The infection can be prevented with sprays, which must begin at the time of the growth flush.

Monilinia of Flowers and Branches

Monilinia increasingly affects sour cherry trees. New varieties, which are resistant to this fungal disease, should be used.

> The varieties Morina, Karneol, or the hybrid cherry Queen Hortensie are less affected and are, therefore, recommended.

Fruit Bursting

The bursting of cherries is caused by humidity. Water penetrates into the fruit through the skin and then tears the skin open. The larger the fruit is, the easier it bursts open and begins to rot. Firm-fleshed varieties are generally more prone to bursting.

Peaches and Nectarines

Aphids

Aphids cause severe leaf rippling with these fruit varieties as well. They are also transmitters of the plum pox virus.

> When the first aphid colonies appear, affected shoots are cut off or treated with organic or synthetic insecticides.

Leaf Curl

The initial symptoms that indicate infection by leaf curl disease are reddish-colored leaves with fleshy protrusions. In the following weeks, the leaves dry up and fall off. Fruits also drop off with heavy defoliation.

Spores, which cause new infections the following year, can be found again in June on buds and shoots. These infections can already occur in February when bud scales open after warm weather conditions.

> This fungal disease is easy to control through preventative copper spraying during winter dormancy.

Infection can also be prevented if a copper compound can be applied just before or after a rainy period.

Gooseberries

Gooseberry Sawflies

Gooseberry sawflies mainly attack gooseberries, but they are also found on red and white currants. There are two species of gooseberry sawflies. The larvae of the yellow and the black gooseberry sawfly, which are about 2/5" to 7/10" long (12-18mm) respectively, eat bushes completely bare during the course of their development. Also, they are considered especially problematic because they can emerge with three, sometimes even four, generations within a vegetation period.

Gooseberry flies are also found on white and red currants.

Getting rid of these pests can definitely reduce the populations, but not successfully control them.

> If an insecticide is used against the first generation, further pest control measures are usually not necessary.

American Gooseberry Mildew

American Gooseberry Mildew is a fungal disease that causes massive damage to shoots as well as fruits. Black currants can also be affected. Control is very difficult. The mycelium of this fungus hibernates in buds. Initial damage can already appear during the growth flush in vulnerable varieties, and is controlled by fungicides with a sequence of sprayings. New breeds have made it possible to grow tolerant varieties that can be used for new plantings.

Currants

Currant Aphid

The currant aphid is widespread in home gardens. This aphid species causes wavy, blister-shaped protrusions that are red-colored. In severe cases, growth rate is also reduced considerably.

The aphids hibernate on the shrubs. After the growth flush, they colonize the bottom of leaves. Over the summer, they leave their host, but return during the fall to lay their eggs.

Treatment with an expellant spray can be carried out during the winter dormant period. Depending on the intensity of the infestation, an organic or synthetic compound can be used to control the aphids.

> Useful insects, such as lacewings or ladybugs, are also very valuable aids for pest control and should not be underestimated.

Currant Gall Mite

Currant gall mites cause severe damage, primarily to black currants. The buds (where the mites hibernate and then reproduce in spring) sprout, but then halt in their development. Later, they dry up and break off. As soon as new buds form, they are colonized by the mites. Damage also occurs on leaves.

Agronomical measures are the main form of pest control.

Affected shoots with round buds are cut off and destroyed. New plantings should be less susceptible varieties.

Infected buds dry up and break off.

Currant Clearwing

The currant clearwing damages not only the currant, but also the gooseberry. The females of this moth lay their eggs near buds from the beginning of June to mid-July. After hatching, they bore themselves into shoots and eat the core. They also hibernate there as pupa.

Affected shoots have a wilted appearance. They are then completely cut off and destroyed.

Blister Rust

Blister rust is primarily found on black currant trees, but damages can also occur on gooseberry trees. The first symptoms of infection are found on the bottom of leaves in the form of yellow blisters. An unhindered spread of this disease can lead to defoliation as early as August.

Blister rust can also appear on gooseberry trees.

Because this fungal disease requires an intermediate host for its development, namely the Weymouth pine, black currants should not be planted near these trees or they should be removed.

A fungicide should be used when the first symptoms appear at the latest. When using other treatments, be sure that waiting periods are observed.

Coral Spot Disease

Coral spot disease mainly affects soft fruits. The spores penetrate into shoots through wounds or injuries, infect the wood, and weaken the growth rate of the shrubs. The damaged shoots should then be cut out.

> In order to prevent an infection, pruning wounds and resulting injuries need to be covered with grafting wax or another compound (artificial bark) so that the spores can no longer invade.

Coulure

The causes of coulure are physiological. In cool, moist weather during bloom, pollination is often inadequate. Furthermore, there is a danger that the female flowering organs freeze in below zero temperatures in the early morning hours. Unsatisfactory pollination can also result from unbalanced shrubs that primarily consist of old fruiting spurs.

Chlorosis

Chlorosis is caused by soil calcium content that is too high. This deficiency disease is resolved by working iron fertilizer into the soil.

Blackberries

Blackberry Gall Mite

Severely cut back the tendrils in the fall!

Blackberry gall mites damage fruit with their feeding activities. Just before the harvest begins, berries stop ripening. They remain partially red and are no longer edible. Because the gall mites hibernate in the affected berries or under bud scales, blackberry tendrils need to be severely cut back in the fall and all damaged fruits destroyed so that another attack during the bloom can be prevented.

> When blackberries begin to bloom and lateral shoots are a few inches/centimeters long, sulfur treatments should be carried out.

Blackberry Rust

Warm, humid weather creates optimal conditions for blackberry rust. Typical characteristics are yellow (and later black-brown) spore clusters on the bottom of leaves. Rusty brown spots appear on the top side. Even before the berries ripen, the damaged leaves fall off and full ripening of the fruits is very insufficient or no longer possible.

Disposing of fallen leaves in autumn is an effective control measure.

If the disease occurs annually, young leaves have to be sprayed with a fungicide in order to prevent infections.

Blackberry rust loves warm, humid weather.

Blackberry Tendril Disease

Visible damage of blackberry tendril disease appears on young tendrils in the summer. Because these don't bloom and bear fruit until the next year, yield losses can occur. The first, barely visible spots continue to spread out and reveal a reddish color.

In the springtime, assimilation disturbances are created by the infection, which disrupt the development of leaves, flowers, and later the small fruits. After a few weeks, the shoots even die off.

Damaged tendrils are completely removed when an infection is discovered.

The development of leaves, flowers, and fruits are disrupted by assimilation disturbances.

Two to three sprays with a copper compound at four-week intervals beginning in April prevent further spread of this disease.

Grapes

Vine Moths

If delicate webs are visible in the young blossoms, this is a sign of an infestation by the first generation of vine moths, also called hay worms. In the summer, the second generation damages the berries — this is known as the sour worm infestation. While the damages in the spring are usually contained, the mass appearance of the sour worm can destroy an entire harvest.

When combating these pests using pheromone traps, the beginning of flight and flight intensity of these moths can be determined.

Organic or synthetic compounds/agents are available as developmental inhibitors.

The second generation causes substantial damage in the summer.

Powdery Mildew

Powdery mildew (Oidium) can already cause infections at the beginning of the growth flush. A mealy, powdery coating on leaves, which can even be wiped off, is a typical symptom of infection. In addition to the leaves, berries and shoots are also affected. Considerable yield losses can be expected with increased appearance. With an infection in the spring, the berries stop growing and dry up. In the summer, the larger berries burst.

> Since the mildew fungus hibernates in buds, a sulfur treatment should be carried out at the time of the growth flush.

In addition to sulfur-based treatments, other synthetic fungicides can also be used over the course of the vegetation period.

Downey Mildew

If oily, transparent spots are visible on the top side of leaves and a white fungal growth on the bottom side, these are symptoms of a downy mildew infection, also called peronospora. Since berries are also affected, a loss in quality can be expected.

Warm weather in connection with rain promotes the infection. Initial damages can already appear after the growth flush.

> Removal of fallen leaves is an important preventative measure of control since the fungal spores develop there. After they germinate, they can attack new leaves and blossoms.

Fungicide treatments with copper compounds or synthetic agents must be carried out as a precautionary measure.

Botrytis

An infestation of botrytis causes areas of decay on grape stems and on the berries. An infection can spread from one berry to the next and a mouse-gray coating of mold forms.

The control measures against this fungal disease are difficult.

> Wound sites, in particular, like those the vine moth can cause, should be avoided.

When the first areas of decay appear, fungicides can at least contain the further spread of botrytis.

Bibliography

Alford, D.-V.: *Farbatlas der Obstschädlinge – Erkennung, Lebensweise und Bekämpfung.* Translated by Steiner, H., Ferdinand Enke Verlag, Stuttgart, 1987.

Beccaletto, J., und Retournard, D.: *Obstgehölze erziehen und formieren.* Verlag Eugen Ulmer, Stuttgart, 2007.

Duhan, K.: *Die wertvollsten Obstsorten – Steinobst I*, Verlag Georg Fromme u. Co., Wien, 1959.

Fischer, M.: *Farbatlas Obstsorten, 2.* stark überarbeitete Auflage, Eugen Ulmer Verlag, Stuttgart 2003.

Friedrich, G., and Petzhold, H.: Handbuch Obstsorten, Eugen Ulmer Verlag, Stuttgart 2005.

Großmann, G., and Wackwitz, W.-D.: Spalierobst, 2. Auflage, Eugen Ulmer Verlag, Stuttgart 2005.

Hartmann, W.: Farbatlas alter Obstsorten, 2. stark überarbeitete Auflage, Eugen Ulmer Verlag, Stuttgart 2003.

de Haas, P.-G.: *Naturgemäßer Obstbaumschnitt, 2.* Auflage, BLV-Verlagsgesellschaft mbH München, München 1973.

Joyce, D.: *Das Große Buch vom Pflanzenschneiden* (original English title: *Pruning and Training Plants*, Mitchell Beazley Publishers, London 1991). German translation Urania Verlag (Verlagsgruppe Dornier), Augsburg.

Jakubik, U.: *Obstbäume schneiden*, Verlag Eugen Ulmer KG, Stuttgart 2005.

Kreuzer, J.: *Kreuzers Gartenlexikon "Kurz und bündig."* Band 3, Gartenbuchverlag, Tittmoning/Obb. 1985.

Löschnig, J., und Passecker, F.: *Die Marille (Aprikose) und ihre Kultur*, Österreichischer Agrarverlag, Wien 1954.

Lucas, F.: *Christ – Lucas Gartenbuch, 19.* Auflage, Verlagsbuchhandlung Eugen Ulmer 1916.

Lütkens, R., and Brickell, Ch. (Hrsg.): *Das große Ravensburger Gartenbuch*, Otto Maier Verlag, Ravensburg 1985.

Muster, G., Strobel, U., Weißmann, K., and Gerlach, H.-K.: *Sortenbeschreibungen Beerenobst*. Staatliche Lehr- und Versuchsanstalt für Wein- und Obstbau Weinsberg, Weinsberg 2004.

Pelzmann, H.: *Kiwi-Kultur*. Leopold Stocker Verlag, Graz 1987.

Scherer, W.: *Schäden an Johannisbeeren und Stachelbeeren erkennen, bestimmen – richtig behandeln*. Pröll Druck und Verlag, Augsburg 1989.

Schipper, A.: *Erfolgreicher Formobstbau*. Gartenbauverlag Trowitzsch und Sohn, Frankfurt/Oder 1940.

Schulz, B., und Großmann, G.: *Obstgehölze erziehen und schneiden*. Verlag Eugen Ulmer, Stuttgart 2002.

Sorge, P.: *Beerenobstsorten, 2. durchgesehene Auflage*. J. Neumann – Neudamm GmbH und Co KG, Melsungen 1991.

Störtzer, M., Wolfram B., Schuricht, W., und Männel, R.: *Steinobst*. Neumann Verlag GmbH, Rodebeul 1992.

Vukovits, G. *Obstkrankheiten – Erkennung, Ursachen und Bekämpfung, Teil II.* Kernobst, Leopold Stocker Verlag, Graz 1980.
Obstkrankheiten – Erkennung, Ursachen und Bekämpfung, Teil III. Steinobst, Leopold Stocker Verlag, Graz 1980.
Obstkrankheiten – Erkennung, Ursachen und Bekämpfung, Teil IV.

Beerenobst, Leopold Stocker Verlag, Graz 1980.

Wesselhöft, J.: *Der Garten des Bürgers und Landmannes, 5.* Auflage, Verlag Beyer und Söhne, Langensalza 1903.

Zech, J.: *Der Obstgarten*, Falken-Verlag Gm.

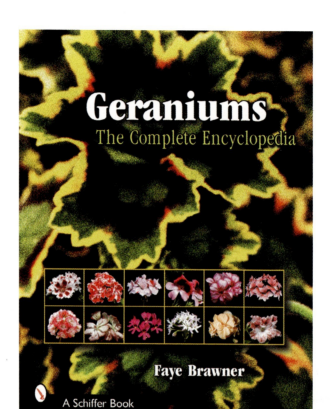

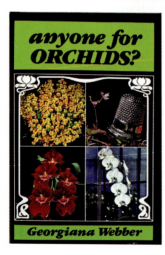

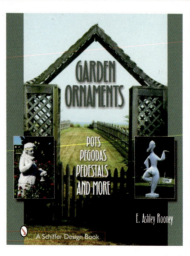

Geraniums: The Complete Encyclopedia. Faye Brawner. Provides detailed background on geraniums (pelargoniums), including scented leaf pelargoniums, zonals, dwarfs, stellars, regals, angels, and more. Hundreds of stunning photographs provide a visual reference of the many colors available. Also includes information on propagation and hybridization, pots and potting soils, food and water, and dealing with diseases and insect pests. A wonderful reference for everyone who enjoys beautiful flowers, on windowsills or in the garden.
Size: 8 1/2" x 11" • 490 color photos • 176 pp.
ISBN: 978-0-7643-1738-5 • soft cover • $19.95

Anyone for Orchids?. Georgiana Webber. A manual of orchid growing, this book covers all you need to know in order to grow the queen of flowering plants, the orchid.
Size: 6" x 9" • 10 line drawings, 24 color plates, 66 b/w photos • 204 pp.
ISBN: 978-0-916838-12-6 • hard cover • $15.00

Garden Ornaments: Pots, Pergolas, Pedestals, and More. E. AshleyRooney. Garden ornaments can breathe life into a garden, no matter its size. This new book presents nearly 500 color photographs of over 350 garden ornaments: animals, maidens, children, miniature trains, urns, gates, pavilions, topiary, birdhouses, and more. Experience an insider's tour of garden ornaments and learn from five notable artists. You may find a favorite garden ornament here, or find the inspiration to create a setting and display your own collection.
Size: 8 1/2" x 11" • 489 color photos • Index • 176 pp.
ISBN: 978-0-7643-1956-3 • hard cover • $34.95

All the Garden's a Stage: Choosing the Best Performing Plants for a Sustainable Garden. Jane C. Gates. Enjoy discovering the hows and whys behind growing a beautiful garden through 293 color images. Learn how to choose the right plants, with tips for lighting, temperature, drainage, and developing a sustainable landscape. This book is great for both the beginner and seasoned gardener, landscape artists, horticulturalists, and everyone who just loves looking at beautiful flowers and plants.
Size: 8 1/2" x 11" • 293 color photos & 40 plans • Index • 144 pp.
ISBN: 978-0-7643-3979-0 • soft cover • $29.99

Schiffer books may be ordered from your local bookstore, or they may be ordered directly from the publisher by writing to:

Schiffer Publishing, Ltd.
4880 Lower Valley Rd.
Atglen, PA 19310
(610) 593-1777; Fax (610) 593-2002
E-mail: Info@schifferbooks.com

Please visit our website catalog at www.schifferbooks.com
or write for a free catalog.

Printed in the China